SOVIET-AMERICAN DANCE MEDICINE

Proceedings of the 1990 Glasnost Dance Medicine Conference and Workshops

Boston, Massachusetts May 18, 19, 1990

Edited by

Lyle J. Micheli, M.D.

Conference Chairman; Director, Sports Medicine Division,

Boston Children's Hospital; President, American

College of Sports Medicine

Ruth Solomon

Professor, University of California, Santa Cruz

John Solomon, Ph.D

Freelance Editor

Co-Sponsors:

**Sports Medicine Division, Children's Hospital
of Harvard Medical School • Boston Ballet •
American College of Sports Medicine •University of
California, Santa Cruz**

Supporters:

**Aircast • Stretchmate • Boston Marathon Sports
Medicine Research Foundation •
Children's Sports Medicine Research Foundation**

Sponsored by the
National Dance Association
an association of the
American Alliance for Health,
Physical Education, Recreation and Dance

© 1991
American Alliance for Health,
Physical Education, Recreation and Dance
1900 Association Drive
Reston, Virginia 22091

ISBN 0-88314-512-X

CONTENTS

iv

FACULTY

Conference Coordinators

Elaine Bauer
Former Principal Dancer, Boston Ballet

Lyle J. Micheli, M.D.
Attending Physician, Boston Ballet; Director, Division of Sports Medicine, Boston Children's Hospital; President, American College of Sports Medicine

Julie A. Power
Administrative Assistant to Dr. Lyle J. Micheli

Ruth Solomon
Professor, Theatre Arts/Dance, University of California, Santa Cruz

Arleen Walaszek, P.T.
Physical Therapist, Boston Ballet and Boston Ballet School

Guest Faculty

Priscilla Clarkson, Ph.D
Department of Exercise Science, University of Massachusetts, Amherst

Linda H. Hamilton, Ph.D
Staff Psychologist, The Miller Health Center Institute for Performing Artists, New York City; Staff Psychologist, Fair Oaks Hospital, Summit, NJ

William Hamilton, M.D.
Orthopaedist to the New York City Ballet, American Ballet Theatre, and the School of American Ballet, New York City; Attending Senior Surgeon, Roosevelt Hospital, New York City

Anna-Marie Holmes
Assistant to Artistic Director, Boston Ballet

Bruce Marks
Artistic Director, Boston Ballet

Sergei Mironov, M.D.
Head, Section of Sports, Dance, Circus, Performance
Medicine, Central Institute of Orthopaedics and
Traumatology, Moscow, USSR

Martha Myers, M.S.
Henry B. Plant Professor of Dance, Connecticut College;
Dean, American Dance Festival

Christine Ploski, P.T., M.S.
Physical Therapist, Boston Ballet Children's Summer
Workshop; Faculty, Marblehead School of Ballet

Daniel S. Rooks, Sc.D.
Exercise Physiologist, Division of Sports Medicine,
Children's Hospital, Boston

Elly Trepman, M.D.
Assistant Professor of Orthopaedics and Rehabilitation,
Yale University School of Medicine, New Haven

Chris Troyanos, A.T.C.
Head Athletic Trainer, Babson College; Charles River
Sports Therapy West, Inc.

Ellen Wallach
Project Director, "Life After Performing"

1

INTRODUCTION

Preface

Lyle J. Micheli, M.D.

The past ten years have seen a dramatic increase of interest in both the care of injured dancers and, more importantly, the prevention of injuries to dancers. This has resulted in the evolution of a new field for the health care professional, that of dance medicine.

While quite a new discipline in North America, the care of dancers and attention to their special needs has a much older legacy in the Soviet Union, paralleling the special role of ballet in the artistic panoply of that nation.

When Bruce Marks and Anna-Marie Holmes conceived the idea of a Soviet-American *glasnost* production of *Swan Lake*, inviting the legendary Natalia Dudinskaya and Konstantine Sergeyev and a coterie of Soviet dancers to join the artistic staff and dancers of the Boston Ballet in this production, the medical team of the ballet saw this as a remarkable opportunity to share information and knowledge with our dance medicine colleagues in the Soviet Union.

In North America, the great majority of the new "dance medicine practitioners" have had prior experience in caring for athletes. The evolution from sports medicine to dance medicine is a logical and easy progression. Quite interestingly, this affinity between the needs and concerns of elite athletes and elite dancers was also well recognized in the Soviet Union. Dr. Sergei Mironov and his colleagues from the Section of Sports, Dance, Circus, Performance Medicine of the Central Institute of Orthopaedics and Traumatology in Moscow have most kindly joined us in this project. As is evident

2

from the title of the clinic that Dr. Mironov directs, the care of dancers and athletes is combined and coordinated in the same therapeutic and rehabilitation facilities in the Soviet Union.

The information shared in this combined conference is, in my opinion, "state of the art" for American medicine and international dance medicine as we enter the '90s. We are very grateful to the artistic staff, dancers, and health care professionals of the Boston, Kirov, and Bolshoi Ballets and the Division of Sports Medicine of the Boston Children's Hospital for their hard work and expertise, which ensured the success of this project.

Opening Remarks

Bruce Marks

The last three years have embodied an endeavor to do what we are doing today— to bring representatives of the United States and the Soviet Union together in a dialogue. The dialogue I intended was a nonverbal one, and you will witness that this evening on the stage of the Wang Center, but during the next two days you are going to discuss something that allows the dialogue to go on, and that is the health of artists, specifically dancers.

I have always believed that the artistic director sets the tone for a company, and thus is responsible for everything that goes on in the company. He/she is responsible for the environment in which the dancers work, and for overseeing their daily lives. I spend a great deal of time with my dancers; we talk a lot, often about things that are personal to them—about their feelings, their attitudes, their hopes and aspirations. All of these things relate directly to their health.

When a dancer comes to you with an injury it is a very tense moment. They believe a great deal of their career hinges on whether they dance that night. I have always told them, "Tonight is not the important night; tomorrow is the important night." I try as a director to think of the future—the individual dancer's future and the company's future. It is comforting in this regard to know that I have on my desk a red telephone—the "Hot Line"—that goes straight to Lyle Micheli's office. When I have to use that line, he and his staff always arrange for our people to be seen immediately.

The exciting part of all this is that there is so much to be learned in terms of what we are doing with our bodies, and what people like Dr. Micheli and his colleagues are doing to help our bodies. With the medical staff behind us, one feels that life at the Ballet can go on, and is secure.

Dance Medicine: An Overview

Lyle J. Micheli, M.D.

What follows is a synopsis of the presentation made by Lyle J. Micheli at the Glasnost Dance Medicine Conference.

I would like to discuss briefly the historic evolution of this conference and of dance medicine. Two days ago a group of six American physicians and experts in the psychology and physical therapy of dance met with six of their Russian counterparts under the auspices of the National Institutes of Health in Washington, DC. We shared information, and we Americans were fascinated to find out about the origins of their dance medicine, which turned out to be quite similar to the evolution of that field in this country. It has developed in parallel with, and benefited from discoveries in, sports medicine.

An obvious question is, why dance medicine? Do dancers have special problems, unique injuries? The answer is an emphatic "yes," as, for example, in stress fractures of the second metatarsal. There are cases such as the one in which a male dancer (something of a diagnostician himself) told me that he was experiencing excruciating pain on the plantar aspect of the sole of his first toe. We examined him this way and that, including the use of fancy bone scans, and could find nothing, which induced me to assume that this was another of his imaginary diseases. Finally one night, backstage, he said "This is really killing me"; I examined him and felt for the first time a small, peculiar lump in his toe. It turned out to be something called an inclusion cyst, which must indeed have been extremely painful. So he was right, and the moral of this story is that with dancers you must trust what they tell you— more, perhaps, than people in any other field—because they know their bodies.

Now dance is changing, and medicine is changing in ways that greatly increase our ability to deal with dance injuries. There are technological advances, for example the MRI, that allow us to image things that two years ago would have escaped us.

There are areas of sports activity and sports medicine that bear many similarities to dance. In gymnastics, for example, many of the maneuvers that endanger gymnasts are common as well to dancers. The legacy of sports medicine, which dates back roughly sixty years in this country (at least to the publication of Thorndike's text book in 1924), can be very beneficial in dealing with dancers. There are studies of figure skaters and gymnasts that can be used as a basis for approaching similar problems in dancers.

The thing we must remember in dance medicine is that

any aspect of medicine requires the classic diagnosis-treat-ment-rehabilitation mode of dealing with injuries. Too often, at present, we see treatment being initiated without a clear diagnosis, and that must never be allowed to happen. This is what Hippocrates told us, in accordance with the Aristotelian approach. I can give you an illustration in the case of a young soccer player who developed a pain in his knee when running, was therefore diagnosed as having "runner's knee" (whatever that is!), and treated with various techniques such as icing and a modification of his soccer shoe. The pain persisted, how-ever, so he came to our clinic. We took x-rays, which looked a little suspicious in the tibia. Ultimately, his "runner's knee" turned out to be an osteogenic sarcoma—a tumor of the proximal tibia. So we need an accurate diagnosis in every case. Finally, rehabilitation means return to function, and we all know that the level of function needed to return a dancer to dance is very different from that involved in most forms of work, or even sports.

Dance medicine research is just in its infancy. People who are interested in dancers—such as ourselves at Children's Hospital, and Dr. William Hamilton in New York, Dr. James Garrick in San Francisco, and Dr. Jim Sammarco in Cincin-nati—are finding ways to study them in a progressive, on-going fashion, trying to find out why these particular injuries occurred, or how we can enhance performance without en-couraging injury. Anyone can do research; research is just applied logic, trying to figure out why something happened, and eliminating those factors which impede or distort our results. We have a need for research in dance medicine, and we must all answer this need. How can we advance training, without risking injury? How much *pointe* work is enough for the young dancer, and how much is too much? Is the modern dancer helped by ballet training or hindered? All are obvious research questions. We will be repeating this need for good basic research as this conference progresses, as well as telling you what we know at the present time about dance injuries and how they occur.

2

PRESENTATIONS

Anatomic, Physiologic, and Developmental Concerns: Dance Injury

Lyle J. Micheli, M.D.

What follows is a synopsis of the presentation made by Lyle J. Micheli at the Glasnost Dance Medicine Conference.

During this conference you will be hearing a great deal about the "what" of dance injuries; in this presentation I am going to focus on <u>why</u> these injuries happen. The reason for concerning ourselves with the "why" of injuries is so that we can back-track from that point, as we do in medicine generally, to see what we can do to prevent these injuries.

Dancers may be subject to some injuries not because of any anatomical abnormality, but as a result of the unusual stresses imposed on their bodies by dance technique. In the young dancer there is a special consideration of growth and development. We are superimposing a dance curriculum on a growing skeleton. Properly done, it can help to enhance normal growth; improperly done, it can cause special kinds of injury.

Injury can occur basically by two different mechanisms, or combinations thereof. Acute macrotraumatic injuries are those that happen, for instance, when a dancer comes down from a jump with the ankle in an excessively inverted position, causing trauma to the outer structure of the ankle. Repetitive microtrauma results from any training regimen that requires repetitive activity. Then there are combinations; if someone has a weakened structure about the knee, for instance, that can contribute to compensatory overuse injury at the ankle of the same extremity.

There are certain anatomic constraints in human beings.

We constantly press the edges of these in dance training: How much is enough? How much is too much? So we have to know anatomy. There are also biologic constraints; exercise physiology has much to teach us here. We are just now beginning to learn how to assess these constraints. When someone comes to our office and asks "How much gymnastics should my 10 year old daughter do?" we barely know the answer. There is some new evidence, determined by researchers working backward from reported injuries, that if you train at gymnastics for more than 16 hours per week you are inviting a whole new level of injuries. In running, all other factors being equal, the comparable figure is approximately 40 miles a week. There are no doubt similar thresholds in dance.

The great laboratory for research on overuse injuries—and much of what we are dealing with in our dancers (and athletes) is overuse injury—was the running boom of the 1970s. This was spurred in part by funding from the running shoe industry, which experienced tremendous increase in sales as a result of the boom. We found out through this research that when you run, a force between three and five times your body weight is sent like a sound wave up the entire extent of your body. This can break tissues in some people. The analogy to the jumps performed by dancers is obvious. The cavalcade of overuse injuries includes stress fracture, tendinitis, chondromalacia, bursitis, and fasciitis.

Children get overuse injuries too, although 20 years ago we had no conception of this. The first mention of a pediatric stress fracture in the medical literature, for example, was in 1951. We now know from dealing with children who do repetitive activity, like dance, that they get a lot of stress fractures and other types of overuse injuries, to which, in fact, they have a special susceptibility.

In answer to our question "Why did that overuse injury occur in that young dancer?" we feel we can identify the following "risk factors," which we now want to look at one by one: training; technique; muscle imbalance; anatomic malalignment; footwear; surface; associated illness; nutrition; cultural deconditioning; psychological stress; and growth. Again, many of our observations will be borrowed from sports medicine information and research.

Training

The effect of rate and intensity of training on injury rate was the subject of an important paper by Dr. Michael Pollock, an exercise physiologist, in 1968. He had one group of adult males run at 70% of VO2 max for 40 minutes, four times a week. They had a 12% rate of overuse injury. A second group, running at 85% of VO2 max for 15 minutes three times a week, had a 22% rate of injury. For a third group, running at 85% of VO2 max 45 minutes three times a week, the rate of overuse injury was 54%. This was the first scientific demonstration of the importance of training as an isolated factor. From running, again, we now know that most of us can safely increase our training regimen by 10% a week. So if you have a young dancer who has been training two hours a day, five days a week, and she goes to a summer program where she is suddenly dancing six hours a day, that is a violation of training progression, and overuse injury may be the result.

Technique

By now we all know that faulty technique, especially in ballet, puts abnormal and excessive stresses on the anatomy. "Sickling in" of the foot, improper performance of the plié in which the pelvis, knee and foot are not aligned, turning out below the knee instead of from the hip—these are some of the common examples of faulty technique that can easily lead to overuse injury.

This last problem, improper turn-out, deserves an extra word. What determines your turn-out is anteversion, or retroversion, of the hip. It is still being debated whether with early, progressive training you can influence this bony alignment. At any rate, the further the femoral neck angle comes forward in its socket, the less turn-out you will have; the more it goes backward, the more you will have true bony retroversion. By the way, as many dancers know, the two hips are not always equal in their ability to produce true turn-out.

Muscle Imbalance

In a study we did some years ago with our dancers from the Boston Ballet we looked at strength of the muscles of the lower extremity. We found, for example, that the hamstring-quadriceps ratio was about 7:4, which is "normal." However, when we looked at the ratio of the muscles that dorsiflex the foot (raise it up) to those responsible for plantar flexion (pushing down, as on to *pointe*), it was dramatically unbalanced toward the latter. We think that may indeed be the culprit in many of the overuse injuries we see about the foot and ankle in dancers. One of our first interventions in dealing with these injuries, after we have taken down any local swelling and relieved pain by the use of ice and anti-inflammatories, is invariably to start strengthening exercises.

One of the questions we often hear in this context is "When should a child go on *pointe*?" Balanchine's answer was probably the best: "When they can do something once they're up there!" You must understand, though, that what he really meant was "when they are strong enough." We have an ongoing study now in which we are looking at strength in kids before they go on *pointe* and a year after they have started *pointe* work, to see if there is any scientific measurement we can find for the required muscle strength in the ankle.

Muscle imbalance can also cause problems at the knee. If the quadriceps muscle is too strong on the outside of the knee, for example, relative to its strength on the inside, it can pull the kneecap out of its normal alignment. That bony structure will then develop an abnormal shape as it remodels itself to adjust to the new position.

Anatomic Malalignment

Frequently young girls who are "pigeon toed" get referred into ballet by well-intentioned people who imagine that those turned-out feet will work to their advantage. Then what we find is that as these girls become increasingly committed to the discipline they are frequently getting injured in the lower extremities. This is an example of how anatomical alignment can contribute to overuse injuries. At this point someone, either a dance teacher or a health professional, has to sit down with the girl's parents and explain why a career in ballet probably is not a good idea for her. I would hope it is becoming increasingly acknowledged in the dance community that teachers do owe it to themselves and to their students to exercise this kind of responsibility.

There has been some misunderstanding in the medical profession as to what constitutes ideal anatomy at the foot and ankle for a dancer. I was at a sports medicine conference some years ago and one of the experts there said, "You can't dance if you have flat feet." We went back and looked at the dancers in the Boston Ballet School, and they all had flat feet; they were all ligamentously lax, but the thing was they could pull their arches up by their muscles. They didn't have fixed flat feet; on the contrary, they had very flexible feet. It turns out that the highly arched "cavus" foot is the one that most often selects people out of dancing.

Footwear and Surface

Footwear and surface: there has been a good deal of research by now in sports medicine and especially in aerobic dance that looks at these factors as contributors to injury. I think we need some of this in ballet, especially toward the development of a ballet shoe that would still conform to the foot, be aesthetically pleasing, allow performance, yet decrease the occurrence of injury.

We still have no scientific criteria of how hard is too hard for a dance surface. We know that surface is a factor in injury, but we still don't know how to measure it.

Associated Illness

What about the dancer who, two weeks into a run of "Nutcracker," develops a bad respiratory illness? She requires special attention because, as we now know, this kind of associated illness is an invitation to dance injury.

Nutrition

There has been a great deal of research on nutrition in dancers. The female dancer in particular seems to be very susceptible to nutritional abnormalities. There is clearly an interaction between such abnormalities and dance activity as a precipitator of overuse injuries. When we have a stress fracture in one of our young female dancers we spend a good deal of time going into her menstrual history and nutritional intake. We do this because we now know that when an athletic young woman loses her normal menses she becomes osteopenic—that is, the calcium content of her bone goes down. As a result , the incidence of stress fractures goes up.

Cultural Deconditioning

Cultural deconditioning is something we tend not to think of too often. For one reason or another many of our children are deprived of proper exercise. The suburban child, for example, who rides the bus to and from school and then locks herself in the house and watches television until her mother comes home in the evening is not getting as much exercise as did her grandmother who was raised on a farm in Nebraska. When we suddenly ask this child to do dance training, or gymnastics, or soccer for one intense hour three to four times a week, it is an invitation to injury, because her tissues have been systematically weakened. This is now very noticeable in our entire urban population. So we have these culturally deprived kids, we put them into dance training, and that can definitely be a factor in dance injury. We probably have to go slower with them.

Psychological Stress

It goes without saying that the dancer who is having trouble with a contract, or similar socioeconomic problems, is at increased risk for injury because of the resulting psychological stress. This also has been demonstrated in various sports medicine studies.

Growth

Finally, in part because we work in a children's hospital, we are particularly concerned with the issue of growth. We know, for instance, that there is a "danger period" in the growth cycle of children. In girls the "adolescent growth spurt" normally occurs between 11-13 years of age; in boys it is a little later, ages 12-14. Because growth takes place in the bone, the soft tissues surrounding the bone—the ligaments and muscle-tendon units—get tighter, and children lose flexibility at the time of rapid growth. This can cause what we traditionally call "growing pains," though I don't much like that term as it is imprecise and can hide diagnoses. We prefer the term "growth risk" to describe this period when the physeal cartilage is growing rapidly, causing weakness in the bone itself as well as the already mentioned tightening of the connective tissues. Perhaps the most dangerous injuries we see at this time, as a result of both macrotrauma and overuse, are those to the growth plates.

I enjoy the work I do in sports medicine, but the area of dance medicine is particularly exciting, because there one is always dealing with the capabilities of the human body taken to the limit. You always have to keep an open mind in dealing with dancers' injuries; you mustn't be too certain that you know exactly why a given injury happened. Just when you think you have life's answers, they change the questions.

Orthopaedic Aspects of Dance Medicine

William Hamilton, M.D.

What follows is a synopsis of the presentation made by William Hamilton at the Glasnost Dance Medicine Conference. This material is copyrighted by him.

The professional ballet dancer is a highly tuned athlete. In a study performed by Nicholas in the mid-1970s, ballet ranked second only to professional football in a list of 63 sports compared for overall difficulty. So what we are looking at in the ballet dancer is a thoroughbred that has been selected out by a Darwinian process for a number of physical qualities: general ligamentous laxity, 180 degrees of turn-out of the lower extremities, 90 degrees of plantar flexion of the foot and ankle, aesthetic body proportions, proper training and technique, and a great capacity for hard work and self-discipline. I would say that only the astronaut is a more selected person in our society.

Where the dance medicine doctor comes into the picture is when dancers try to do things that even they can't get away with; if you push any system long and hard enough you will eventually find its weak link. If you examine the selected ballet dancer you will usually find, for example, that they have a reduced turn-in at the hip; the normal measurement in the prone position is approximately 40 degrees, whereas these dancers often have as little as 15 degrees of internal rotation. This can lead to problems; when the dancers of the New York City Ballet are asked to do modern dance, for instance, we immediately begin to get injuries.

There is a great deal of thickening of the metatarsal bones in female ballet dancers. This is Wolfe's Law of bone responding to the stressors placed on it. These bones have to be more dense than normal to bear the weight of the body on *pointe* and *demi-pointe*, and developing that density is a slow process. This is one of the reasons why ballerinas have to start dancing early, so changes in their skeletal structure can occur while they are growing and while their body weight is gradually increasing. Thus everything works in concert. You get into trouble when you try to circumvent this process. Fractures of the metatarsals and (more commonly in modern dancers) of the sesamoids, necrosis of the sesamoids, and Frieberg's disease are some of the possible problems. The most common fracture in female dancers (the so-called "dancer's fracture") is a spiral oblique fracture of the fifth metatarsal, which usually results when the dancer loses her balance while *en pointe* and falls over the outer border of the foot.

Because of the recurvatum of the knee in the ballet leg, an extreme amount of plantar flexion is required in the foot-ankle complex. To carry that down a joint further, in order to dance on *demi-pointe* the dorsiflexion needs to be 100-110 degrees at the axis of the first metatarsal, as compared to a norm of 40 degrees. This requires another molding process on the growing skeleton. Older dancers can build up bone spurs and impingements slowly over the dorsum of the joint, and surgery to clean that out can extend careers. In the younger dancer this often takes the form of a sort of Osgood-Schlatter's disease, an inflammation of the first MTP joint as a result of micro-fractures sustained in the process of molding the joint. It responds to rest, though it may recur, and generally disappears when growth is completed.

Bunions are quite common, and should never be surgically removed in the population of which we are speaking, as there is no way you can remove a bunion and leave that required 100 degrees of dorsiflexion.

A very characteristic stress fracture is seen at the base of the second metatarsal, where it is recessed into the middle cuneiform which forms the keystone of a very strong "Roman arch." As Dr. Micheli has pointed out, interarticular fractures can also occur in this area. So you have to be very suspicious of pain at the base of the second metatarsal. Dancers have a very high arch which can distort the normal x-ray in this area, so in our office we take x-rays of the second metatarsal upside down, with the top of the foot against the x-ray plate ("the dancer's view"). In this way it is possible to pick up little chip fractures that otherwise might be missed.

Tarsal coalitions are unions between bones that shouldn't be there. We might select a prospective dancer who has these (as detected by the use of MRI) out of dance, as they restrict the required sub-talar rotation.

The *grand plié* that is so essential to ballet will carve a deep trough in the neck of the talus. Especially in male dancers who do a lot of bravura dancing this is often accompanied by bone spurs that build up in the front of the ankle. Again, older dancers frequently need to have this cleaned out. The bone scan is especially useful in picking up this kind of condition, and also osteoid osteoma.

The equinus, or plantar flexed position, leads to problems behind the ankle. There are two major syndromes that occur in that location: posterior lateral pain, which is by the fibular, and posterior medial pain, on the inside of the ankle. If an os trigonum is present, it limits the plantar flexion that is possible in the talus. This does not invariably cause trouble because by starting young the dancers can sublux their mid-tarsal joints, and thereby compensate for the loss of plantar flexion.

There are two tubercles in the back of the ankle, the lateral and medial tubercles. The former of these is the origin of the posterior talo-fibular ankle ligament, and in between the two tubercles runs the flexor hallucis longus tendon, which eventually goes to the big toe and, for the ballet dancer, is the main support and strength tendon in the foot. Much posterior lateral pain is caused by os trigonums that form at the back of the heel. When this impingement occurs behind the ankle it can cause the ankle to wedge open at the front, so the entire weight of the body is carried down into the foot through a minimal area of contact. Fractures of the os trigonum can occur, and all kinds of anatomical abnormalities.

There is also the "loose ankle," which has a third degree instability as a result of multiple sprains. What happens is that the ankle ligaments are not able to hold the talus back under the tibia when the dancer *relevés,* and when that happens the tibia comes down to rest on the os trigonum. So the cause of the impingement in this case is the loose ankle syndrome, and the treatment is to tighten the ankle ligaments, and not go in and explore the back of the ankle.

You can have posterior impingement without any bony structure back there. There is a "pseudo meniscus" that can be torn, similarly to what happens in the knee, and it then locks and gives way.

That flexor hallucis longus tendon, again, can cause lots of trouble where it passes through its fibro-osseous tunnel, like a rope through a pulley. It tends to get swollen and bind, and can become strained and even develop knots. These conditions cause the big toe to trigger. Usually they heal by conservative therapy; you hardly ever have to operate. When you do have to open one up what you find is constriction at the entrance to the tunnel where the muscle fibers are being pulled in. The dancers who have this problem suffer from a functional hallux rigidus; when the ankle is in plantar flexion, dorsiflexion of the big toe is present, but when the ankle is pushed into dorsiflexion, the big toe becomes rigid.

A few words about ankle sprain: We grade ankle sprains in three degrees of severity. Grade 3 is "loose as a goose"; grade 1 is barely discernible; and grade 2 is everything in between. Fortunately, in dancers grade 3 sprains are very rare. The order in which the ligaments are torn depends on the position the ankle is in at the time of injury. If the ankle is in dorsiflexion, then the calcaneal fibular ligament is under tension and the anterior talo-fibular ligament is relaxed, so the former tends to tear. When that happens, there is always some sub-talar instability in addition to the instability at the ankle itself. Dancers, though, are almost always in plantarflexion, so they tend much more often to tear the anterior talo-fibular ligament. Most of these tears can be treated by conservative therapy and rehabilitation. When there is a third degree tear in a dancer, though, it usually requires surgery, as that injury doesn't heal well otherwise.

The most important thing in dealing with sprains is to strengthen the peroneals. If you push against a dancer's foot in a *tendu*, they should be able to resist no matter how hard you push. If the ankle gives way, then the peroneals are weak, and need to be strengthened in full plantar flexion on a home regimen. You should always take an AP x-ray of the foot with all ankle injuries, because you can have associated problems. The diagnosis of the sprained ankle that won't get better is a very complex matter. The number one cause is unrecognized peroneal weakness, which leads to rotatory instability, or you can have that posterior impingement that I spoke about before, or posterior process fracture, flexor hallucis tendinitis, or problems around the tip of the fibular. Fracture of the anterior process of the os-calcus is commonly associated with ankle sprain.

In the two ballet companies I work with we have cut problems of the Achilles tendon in half by use of a simple "stretch box." Rupture of the Achilles tendon does occasionally occur, however, especially in older dancers. This used to end careers, but nowadays that needn't be the case. The critical thing in repairing this injury is to get the tendon the same length it was before it tore. That is really the reason to operate, as the tendon *will* heal without surgery. If you get the tendon too short, the dancer can't *plié*; if it is too long, they can't jump. You have to warn the dancer, at any rate, that they will be unable to dance for a year with this repair.

In dancers the main knee problems involve the patella, because the knee is caught in between the turned in hip and the turned out foot. This causes a marked increase in the Q-angle, which in turn causes the patella to slip out of its groove. Therefore, the first thing to look at in a dancer who is having knee problems is their turn-out. I examine them in the prone position, and more often than not what I find is that they don't really have good turn-out.

Arthritis to the hip is a common problem in older dancers. One of the causes, I am certain, is acetabular dysplasia. Many dancers have hips that contain the seeds of their own destruction, because although they have excellent turn-out and fabulous range of motion, they have dysplastic sockets that allow the head of the femur to slip too far out, and this damages the labrum and the anterior lip of the acetabulum. Therefore, in any dancer who is having recurrent strains of the hip, you must do a complete evaluation with x-rays.

Scoliosis is extremely common. In our studies there is a 50% incidence in the dancers of the New York City Ballet and American Ballet Theater. Even more surprising, one finds this same percentage in males. There is no telling what will happen with these curves, so no matter how large or small they may be they need to be followed closely by an orthopaedist. All dance teachers need to know about this, as early diagnosis (and aggressive treatment when indicated) is the hallmark of dealing with this problem.

Spondylolysis, which is a stress fracture of the back, presents with unilateral lumbo-sacral back pain that in dancers hurts on one side when they *arabesque*, but not the other. Often this condition will show on bone scans even when not present in x-rays. If picked up and treated early, it will often heal itself, though bracing may sometimes be required.

The important thing to remember is that despite all this anatomy, with dancers what is happening on the inside is never so important as what is happening on the outside.

Stress Fractures in the Dancer

Elly Trepman, M.D.

What follows is a paper written by Dr. Trepman, upon which his presentation at the Glasnost Dance Medicine Conference was based.

A stress fracture is a discontinuity in the normal structural integrity of bone, which usually does not involve the entire diameter of the bone. Stress fractures occur after a recent change in activity and are characterized clinically by the insidious, gradual development of pain, without any history of single-impact injury. Localized swelling may occur in addition to pain, and physical examination reveals discrete tenderness at the site of the fracture. Radiographs may be normal.

Historically, stress fractures have been classified etiologically as either fatigue fractures or insufficiency fractures. The fatigue fracture is an overuse injury that results from repetitive microtrauma, and may occur in normal bone. Insufficiency fractures are stress fractures that occur in bone intrinsically weakened by physiological problems such as hormone imbalance. In the dancer, stress fractures may be caused by either or both of these factors.

The first description of a stress fracture has been attributed to Breithaupt, a Prussian military surgeon.[1] Much of our current understanding of stress fractures has resulted from work in the military, in which the incidence of stress fractures ranges from 5 to 30%. The large numbers of recruits partici-

21

pating in the standardized activities of basic training, in which there is a sudden change in intensity and character of activity, have allowed for statistically significant epidemiological studies of stress fractures. Such studies are less feasible in dance companies, which are smaller and less standardized, but concepts developed in the military and other sports populations about stress fracture biology may be applied to dancers.

Stress fractures in dancers were first reported in 1956 by Burrows.[2] Five dancers had presented with tibial pain, particularly with leaps. Biopsy was required in two for diagnosis because the nature of the problem was not well known, and more sophisticated imaging techniques were not yet available. Microscopic examination of the biopsy specimens revealed many channels of resorbed dead bone, adjacent to a frank crack in the bone (the stress fracture defect).[2] When bone is injured, special cells (osteoclasts) create these channels by removing the dead bone in preparation for new, healing bone formation. The channels or holes formed during this resorption process result in weakening of the bone, making it more susceptible to fracture.

Normal bone responds to repetitive stress by adaptive thickening of the cortex, thus increasing the ability of the bone to withstand more stresses. An elegant biomechanical study of ballet dancers *en pointe* demonstrated that in feet with a longer second toe, more pressure is carried by the second toe compared with feet having a shorter second toe.[3] Dancers with long second metatarsal bones develop cortical thickening of this bone,[4] presumably because of the increased load carried by the long second metatarsal in *relevé* and *en pointe*. Furthermore, in a study of ballet dancers who had radiographs of the entire lower extremity, the vast majority had cortical thickening of the tibia, femur, and first three metatarsals, and over half of the dancers had radiographic evidence of stress fracture of the femoral neck.[5]

Pathogenesis

Stress fractures occur when a new pattern of repetitive stress is applied to a bone. Cyclical loads result in repetitive microtrauma, which in bone manifests as microscopic cracks.

These cracks may occur within 10-12 days after beginning a new activity, such as rehearsing a new piece of choreography. If the repetitive loads are stopped, these cracks may heal before symptoms develop. However, if the new activity is continued, then the microtrauma may progress, weakening the bone. Furthermore, during the third week after the change in activity, the mechanical strength of the bone is also weakened by the development of resorption channels. The healing response, which consists of new bone formation around the outer (periosteal) surface of the bone, usually occurs during the fourth week after the microtrauma.[6] If the bone is sufficiently weakened by the ongoing microtrauma and the associated resorption process, before the healing response occurs, then stress fracture will result.

The timing of these events is critically important. Bone is weakest during the third week after the onset of a new training program, when microscopic cracks and resorption channels have progressed, and before new periosteal healing bone is formed. This knowledge was applied, with dramatic results, in one study of military trainees at Fort Knox, Kentucky.[7] The basic training program was modified by eliminating repetitive impact activities, such as running and jumping, from the third week of training. This single modification in timing of repetitive impact activities resulted in a 67% reduction of stress fracture incidence compared with trainees in the unmodified program. This attention to timing should also be applicable to dancers.

Risk Factors

The risk factors for overuse injury, previously discussed by Dr. Micheli, are important for the understanding of how stress fractures occur in dancers, and how they may be prevented. The factors that contribute to the occurrence of stress fractures in dancers include the following:

1. Training error, either in quantity or quality. When the intensity or duration of an activity is progressed too rapidly, before musculoskeletal adaptation can occur, stress fracture may result. In dance, this may occur during an intensive summer training program, or after a layoff period. When the

type of activity is modified without gradual progression, such as with a change in choreography or promotion from *corps* to solo work, the dancer is at increased risk for stress fracture.

2. Technical errors may increase repetitive stress on particular bones. Excessive lumbar lordosis during extension activities or lifts may increase the stresses on specific parts of the spine, resulting in spondylolysis. Other technical errors such as "screwing" the knees to increase apparent turn-out, or "sickling" the feet, may increase stresses in the lower extremity. Diverse dance techniques may alter injury pattern because of different musculoskeletal stresses.[8]

3. Anatomical factors, such as tight lumbar lordosis, femoral anteversion, or cavus feet, may alter the pattern of musculoskeletal stresses and contribute to the development of stress fractures. Military trainees with more than 65 degrees of external rotation of the hip had a twofold greater stress fracture rate than those with less hip turn-out;[9] the opposite would be expected in dance activity, and similar studies of body alignment, structure, and joint motion in dancers may reveal other anatomic risk factors.

4. Muscle imbalance may impair the shock absorption and deceleration functions of muscles and may increase the stresses on bones. Impaired strength or flexibility, insufficient warmup, or muscle fatigue may all contribute to injury.

5. Footwear characteristics may alter stress patterns on the lower extremities. The different injury patterns between dance styles may, in part, be a result of different shoewear, such as the *pointe* shoe in ballet, spiked heel shoe in jazz dance, or bare foot in modern dance. As previously demonstrated in runners, improvements in shoe characteristics, such as impact absorption and support, may decrease injury, and similar research is needed to improve dance shoes.

6. Hormonal and nutritional status. Dancers with hypoestrogenism, manifested by delayed menarche or secondary amenorrhea, have an increased risk of stress fracture.[10]

7. Dance floor design is critically important. Good floor characteristics include proper surface friction, resiliency, and shock absorption, and may reduce muscle fatigue and impact stresses.

8. The role of genetics is less well known. Caucasian and black military trainees have different rates of stress fracture. In one instance, identical twin military trainees sustained identical stress fractures of the femur and talus, suggesting a genetic predisposition.[11]

9. Growth. Stress fractures of the growth plate have been described. The decrease in flexibility during the adolescent growth spurt may result in increased stress both on bones and on the site of insertion of tendons to bone.

10. Associated disease state. Previous injury may cause weakness and stiffness that may contribute to the development of stress fracture. Problems such as osteoarthritis may increase stresses on the bones adjacent to the affected joints.

Diagnosis

The dancer with a stress fracture usually complains of localized pain of gradual onset, and there may be a recent change in activity level. Physical examination reveals discrete tenderness at the fracture site. Radiographs may be normal in the early stages, or may reveal a small fracture line or an area of periosteal, healing new bone formation.

The technetium radionuclide bone scan is the most sensitive diagnostic test for stress fracture, and is often performed if the plain radiographs are negative. The radionuclide is injected intravenously and circulates to the bones, where it is concentrated in areas of increased vascularity such as fractures. The disadvantages of the test include the requirement of an injection, the waiting period of several hours after the injection before the study can be completed, and the radiation exposure equivalent to that of several radiographs. However, the bone scan has greatly helped with the early diagnosis and reduction of morbidity from stress fractures.

A relatively new diagnostic test, magnetic resonance imaging (MRI), may be helpful in the future for the diagnosis of stress fracture.[12] This noninvasive technique uses magnetism—not ionizing radiation—to reveal body tissue structure. It may be oversensitive in some instances by revealing minor problems such as bone bruises, and currently is too expensive for routine use.

Anatomic Sites

Stress fractures in the dancer most commonly occur in the foot and ankle, tibia and fibula, femur and hip, and spine. In the foot, the base (proximal end) of the second metatarsal is commonly involved, where the second metatarsal is stabilized at the tarsometatarsal (Lisfranc) joint, because this is where much stress concentration occurs *en pointe* and in *relevé*. Stress fracture of the second and third metatarsal neck, fifth metatarsal, navicular, and cuneiform bones may also occur. Sesamoid stress fractures result from dancing on a hard floor, against which the sesamoids may be jammed in *relevé*.

The distal fibula is a common site of stress fracture in the dancer. The talus is wider in the front than in the back; therefore, in *plié*, the talus tends to drive the tibia and fibula apart. This action is resisted just above the level of the ankle joint by the tibiofibular ligaments, resulting in stress concentration and fracture of the fibula at this location. Treatment includes avoidance of *plié*.

The tibia shaft, femur, and femoral neck are common sites of stress fracture in the dancer. The most common stress fracture in the spine is spondylolysis, at the pars interarticularis between the facet joints. Stress fracture of an arthritic facet joint may occur in the veteran dancer, but the lumbar pedicle is only rarely affected.

Treatment

The goals of treatment include a healed fracture, and a dancer who has returned to unlimited, painless, and safe function. Stress fractures are treated with "relative rest." Impact activities are avoided, as are specific motions that aggravate the particular fracture. For example, *plié* is avoided in stress fracture of the distal fibula, extension work in spondylolysis, and any repetitive standing work in stress fractures of the foot. Restricted weight bearing, braces, or casts are only very rarely required, but the Boston back brace is often helpful in the treatment of spondylolysis.

Maintenance of strength and flexibility, and a gradual return to dance activity, are important in preventing a recurrence of the stress fracture or other overuse injury. This may be achieved with a directed rehabilitation program, swimming activities, and appropriate floor work. Most stress fractures heal in eight weeks, but delayed union or nonunion may occur. If the dancer who has stress fracture ignores the pain and continues in vigorous dance activity, the fracture may progress to a complete fracture—a rare but serious complication.

The treatment program should include an analysis of risk factors which may have caused the current fracture in order to prevent recurrence.

References

1. Breithaupt: Zur pathologie des menschlichen fusses. *Medicin Zeitung* 24:169-171, 175-177, 1855.

2. Burrows HJ: Fatigue infraction of the middle of the tibia in ballet dancers. *J Bone Joint Surg* 38B:83-94, 1956.

3. Teitz CC, Harrington RM, Wiley H: Pressure on the foot in pointe shoes. *Foot Ankle* 5:216-221, 1985.

4. Pelipenko VI: On peculiarities of the development of the foot skeleton in the pupils of a choreographic school. *Arkh Anat Gistol Embriol* 64:46-50, 1973.

5. Schneider HJ, King AY, Bronson JL, Miller EH: Stress injuries and developmental change of lower extremities in ballet dancers. *Radiology* 113:627-632, 1974.

6. Engh CA, Robinson RA, Milgram J: Stress fractures in children. *J Trauma* 10:532-541, 1970.

7. Scully TJ, Besterman G: Stress fracture—a preventable training injury. *Milit Med* 147:285-287, 1982.

8. Solomon RL, Micheli LJ: Technique as a consideration in modern dance injuries. *Physician Sportsmed* 14(8):83-90, 1986.

9. Giladi M, Milgrom C, Stein M, Kashtan H, Margulies J, Chisin R, Steinberg R, Kedem R, Aharonson Z, Simkin A: External rotation of the hip—a predictor of risk for stress fractures. *Clin Orthop Rel Res* 216:131-134, 1987.

10. Warren MP, Brooks-Gunn J, Hamilton LH, Warren LF, Hamilton WG: Scoliosis and fractures in young ballet dancers. *N Engl J of Med* 314:1348-1353, 1986.

11. Singer A, Ben-Yehuda O, Ben-Ezra Z, Zaltzman S: Multiple identical stress fractures in monozygotic twins. *J Bone Joint Surg* 72-A:444-445, 1990.

12. Lee JK, Yao L: Stress fractures: MR imaging. *Radiology* 169:217-220, 1988

Dance Medicine in the Soviet Union

Sergei Mironov, M.D.

What follows is a synopsis of the presentation made by Sergei Mironov at the Glasnost Dance Medicine Conference.

My dear colleagues: First, I would like to thank Dr. Micheli for inviting us to this conference, which is providing us an opportunity to greatly expand our knowledge in the area of science, and also our contacts on a human level.

I want in my remarks today especially to help combat the impression that dancers are constantly sick and traumatized people.

I would like to say a few words about the organization of medical help available to dancers in the Soviet Union. It seems to me that both from the perspective of prevention and of care it is less well organized than for most other forms of sport. On the other hand, there is a system of medical dispensaries that has been set up and made available to the principal dance companies, such as the Bolshoi and Kirov. Since the 1960s these facilities have been providing routine examinations, diagnostic services, and medical treatment to the company members. As far as traumatology and orthopaedics are concerned, the main clinic for dancers is ours in Moscow, which was founded in 1952; more recently, branches have been established in Riga and Leningrad. Our clinics are involved in applied work, such as performing orthopaedic operations, but we also do training of new physicians in the fields of sports and dance medicine, as well as retraining for generalists in these subspecializations.

Regarding the problems that orthopaedists are confronted with, in our opinion most of them originate in childhood, and therefore the selection process by which children are admitted to the ballet schools is actually the starting point of the problem. The selection committees that choose children for admission to the schools do not include any medical personnel; hence, they do not notice (or even look for) the anatomical anomalies that are very likely to lead to problems. To the contrary, they actually interpret certain conditions, such as laxity at the joints, as advantageous to the prospective student. Some of these problems that might seem minor when the dancer is just starting out can become quite major later on. So from our point of view the prime factor in preventing injuries is that there should be very close cooperation between the medical profession and the dance world.

We find that there is a direct link between the nature and quality of the dance school and the type and frequency of traumas experienced by its students. A school with a good preventive program will definitely reduce the injuries that would otherwise occur.

I turn now to some more specific points and clinical observations. First, some problems of the spine. Dysplasia is the background against which many problems of the spine happen. We use a special "scintigraphic" technique to view the various aspects of the spine, with radionucleotide uptake in the bone scan correlated to patterns of inflammation of the soft tissue as demonstrated by computerized thermograms of the spine.

Often when ballet dancers begin to train and perform in a different style they experience back pains. We noticed this a couple of years ago in the ballet schools. With such pains the problem can be attributed to a "discoordination" as a result of changing familiar movement patterns. To deal with such problems we must encourage relaxation and "professional readaptation". We use certain exercise and restoration techniques, both passive and those that involve manual manipulation and massage. There is a whole series of exercises for the muscles that stabilize the back. We especially emphasize "unloaded" exercises, in which there is no weight on the back, and those which emulate actual dance movement. Many of these are done sitting or lying down.

Regarding the knee, most of the problems we encounter involve instability of the patella. We have developed a diagnostic algorithm or pattern in order to define the nature of the particular instability and thereby devise an appropriate treatment modality. At the first stage of dislocation of the patella we always use a conservative treatment. We try to build up those muscles that control lateral movement of the kneecap. If we get unsatisfactory results with the conservative mode of treatment, then we might go on to operative procedures. In cases where we have repetitions of the patella injury we use a procedure that involves only soft tissue. A ligament 15-18 centimeters in length is prepared from the medial retinaculum of the knee and is transplanted. One end is attached at the base of the femoral quadriceps. It is wrapped around the tendons of the patella and re-attached at the pes anserinus tendon. A "double suture" of synthetic material is used in order to create as durable a connection as possible. When the soft-tissue implantation is insufficient, we do what we can to stabilize the knee by using the existing ligaments.

A few words about problems of the Achilles tendon. This is a major problem area for dancers. Just in recent years we have had 91 patients with this pathology at our clinic. There are various methods of operation in cases of complete rupture of the Achilles tendon. One involves simple suturing of the tendon tissue. When that is impossible, however, we might transplant tendon tissue from other parts of the body. Sometimes, especially with dancers 32 years of age and over, we use a "closed" technique of intervention. We place threads in the proximal and distal ends of the tendon. Then, with the foot in the plantar flexed or *pointe* position, we tie the threads together.

Another common Achilles injury is usually described in the literature, especially in the United States, as "tendinitis," but we think that is not a good description of what is happening. We think this is often not a problem with the tendon itself, but of the tendon sheath surrounding it. Part of the problem with this condition is that in its early stages dancers often use steroids injected directly into the tendon tissue to reduce the pain. This leads to necrotic condition in the tendon, and sometimes to its pathological breakdown. We operate to remove scar tissue from along the entire length of the tendon sheath and free the underlying tendon from the sheath.

I don't want to tire you further with this kind of clinical detail. My colleagues and I thank you for inviting us to this conference, which has served as a most enlightening platform for the exchange of information from our two countries.

The Role of Physical Therapy in Dance Medicine

Arleen Walaszek, P.T.

What follows is a synopsis of the presentation made by Arleen Walaszek at the Glasnost Dance Medicine Conference.

What is the role of physical therapy in dance medicine? Superficially this question yields an easy answer: The role of physical therapy is to engage two people in working toward a single goal, and as applied to dance medicine that goal is invariably to return the dancer to dancing. A problem arises only when the dancer and/or the artistic staff to which he/she is responsible asks <u>when </u>will this goal be achieved? Unfortunately, this question seldom yields a standard answer; the individual case must always be considered on its own terms.

Two tools have been helpful to me in my work as a physical therapist. The first is an ability to listen. Proper listening requires a good deal of patience and usually a quiet atmosphere. Actually, like most physical therapists I listen best with my hands. The second tool is an open-mindedness, a willingness to treat each case as though I had never seen anything like it before. This guarantees me a constant supply of surprises, and that makes of physical therapy something very beautiful.

Indeed, no two cases are ever the same. When a patient comes to me he/she brings a diagnosis from the physician, which can lead us to believe that we know from past experience exactly what to do. I have found it beneficial, however, to remain open to fresh, creative solutions.

There are three things that take place in every physical therapy session, with some overlapping and interweaving: evaluation, education, and treatment. Evaluation begins with history-taking, which is repeated as an on-going process at the beginning of each successive session. Two other major considerations in evaluating the patient are flexibility and alignment. Another is the quality of movement: Does it look efficient and graceful? This is really important in dancers.

Dancers are especially amenable to education; they have a very keen sense of wanting to know what their bodies are all about. Anatomy, body mechanics, and personal limitations (and strengths) are often subjects of discussion. Common sense is an element in education: If you can't walk today, I point out to them, it is unlikely you will be able to dance tonight. Also, we talk about common care—the simple things they can do for themselves to improve their situation. We are fortunate at Children's Hospital in that our sessions usually last an hour, which provides ample time for this kind of education.

The third thing, of course, is treatment. Here we have all kinds of modalities we can use, from ultra sound, to electro-stimulation, to massage. My personal preference is hands-on work stressing muscular inhibition and re-education, as well as postural realignment. I am not really a "machine person"; I try to use my hands as much as possible. I am also big on exercises. Perhaps most importantly, I think it is necessary to keep a session light, to ease the burden for a dancer of dealing with his/her pain. I try to make it fun.

As an example of all this, let us consider how we might deal with a young female dancer who comes to us with a referral as a result of increased lordosis and occasional back pain. She has been evaluated by the physician. Her x-ray and bone scan are negative. Normally the referral will indicate something like pelvic strengthening and flexibility, and postural realignment. Basically, we are being asked to devise a therapy that will allow us to keep this young person dancing in good health.

In taking a history the first thing I want to know is does it hurt now, as that will determine how (in what posture) I will perform my evaluation. Then I want to know when it hurts:

every time they dance? only when jumping? only with certain moves? Does it hurt when they <u>don't</u> dance? only in the morning? only when they have a test in school? This line of questioning will begin to tell us how difficult a problem we are dealing with, and how often we will need to see the patient. The other thing I want to know is does anything in particular help: heat? taking a few days off from dance? modifying the class to eliminate some movements? decreasing the turn-out?

The diagnosis in this case is occasional low back pain, so we begin to think right away about what might cause this: Is it a lack of flexibility? Is it the way she is holding herself? Is she shortening the low back? If it is a problem of dance technique I might have to bring in a dance educator to help me.

We look at the position of the head: Is it really far forward, or is it being pulled down and back along with the shoulders, or as the shoulders are being pulled up and forward? Even as I am looking I can begin to educate by telling the patient that what I want her to do is think about lengthening through the back of her head and neck. The next thing I look for is leaning: Is she leaning into the front of her hips and the backs of her knees? If so, re-education involves backing out of the hips and coming up over straight legs. The other thing we look at is whether the ribs are soft, and relaxed, and not being pulled up. If a dancer is told to "pull up," typically she will pull the ribs up, and that causes shortening in the low back. We can often help to avoid elevation of the ribs by educating the patient to breathe properly.

Another reason for low back pain would be if she were clenching in the gluteals. The tell-tale sign of this is "dents" on the side of the hip. Gluteal clenching locks or restricts the exact area that needs to be open to movement and breadth. The educational process has to do with teaching the dancer to relax the gluteals, allowing the pelvis to drop down naturally into a neutral position. Finally, we want to see if she is standing exclusively on her forefoot. If so, we need to correct her weight distribution by bringing it more evenly over the entire foot.

We can evaluate her lower extremity flexibility and check for tightness in the hip sockets in the supine position as well as in standing. For a dancer it is important to know whether they can unfold easily into extension, without holding in the hip sockets. With the young dancer, of course, we hope to find at least 90 degrees of straight leg raising (flexion). If the dancer is overusing the muscles on the front of the hip and thigh in *développé* a stressful muscular pattern will be established and may well inhibit the extension (elevation) of the leg to the front and side. We use the Thomas test to determine that the dancer has complete hip extension, done one leg at a time.

Even if we have found no dominant problem through our evaluation we can assume that a major part of our treatment approach will involve pelvic stretching and strengthening. This means addressing ourselves through exercises to the iliopsoas system. Usually the patient takes home a list of such exercises to practice until the next appointment. In this type of case, a return visit in approximately one month would be appropriate. At that time we would re-evaluate their status, review their program, and make changes as needed.

Workshop: Physical Therapy and Dance

Arleen Walaszek, P.T.

What follows is a synopsis of the presentation made by Arleen Walaszek at the Glasnost Dance Medicine Conference.

Let me say at the outset that the exercises I use in rehabilitating dancers are derived in large part from Ruth Solomon's work. So you will notice a good deal of overlap in what we talk about today and what you saw in her video earlier.

Now, this is to be purely a workshop in which I respond to your needs, so does anyone want to ask about a body part, or a dance problem, or anything of that sort?

Question: In my practice I have seen quite a few modern dancers with lower back problems, and I happen to have trouble in that area myself. In that context, I was appreciative of the attention Ruth gives to the iliopsoas muscle. That is a very deep and powerful muscle, and it has been my experience that most doctors don't really know what to do with it as it is not available to many therapeutic modalities. I would be interested in knowing more about how you (and Ruth) work with it.

Answer: Our approach is based on restrengthening. The first thing we would do is talk about breathing into that area, allowing it to expand with the breath, so as to break up any holding in the rib cage. So I have the dancer lie on his/her back, with the knees bent and heels drawn up close to the ischia, and place my hand under the lumbar area. Then I have him/her press against my hand by going into a gentle undercurve. If there is a serious low back problem I will concentrate for some time on this flexing movement before introducing the extension that we get in the overcurve. This depends, of course, on exactly where the pain is located. Some low back pain can be caused by excessive holding of the tendons on the front of the hip, which we can relieve by stretching them in extension, but more often we want to concentrate on flexion first.

Then we bring the knees up toward the chest and balance them loosely over the torso and hips, with the lower legs parallel to the floor. This releases the iliopsoas, the sartorius, and the rectus. The second part of that exercise is to extend the lower legs from the knee, not necessarily into the extreme hyperextension of which professional dancers are capable, but just to where they are comfortable. Then we rock the pelvis by pressing down in the lumbar spine to move the legs up toward the head. If they can't do this without tightening in the abdominals, then I have them hold with their hands behind the lower legs, and assist the motion that way. We do this initially in first position, and then somewhat opened out toward second, but not to any extreme. I want to be particularly sure that they are working through the lumbo-sacral spine and that the abdominals are relaxed.

Once you get to this point and everything is going well, the next (and last) step is to bring them to a sitting position on the "balance point," which is usually located between the sacrum and the coccyx, with loose hip sockets and released rib cage. Then they might do extensions, one leg at a time, working deeply into the hip sockets.

Question: How do you get more extension in an overly flattened back?

Answer: Well, we allow the overcurve, but also there is much to be said for doing the extension in the supine position, as opposed to standing, where you have to take the weight of the leg up. So, lying on the back with knees bent (heels drawn in), we roll up into a bridge, vertebra by vertebra, to the top.

Then, opening wide across the pelvis, we lower the coccyx, creasing deep in the hip sockets and allow the spine to relax back onto the ground.

Another good exercise begins in the prone position. Working one leg at a time, you lever down through the ilium to flex the knee, then lever down again to lift the leg, and cross the foot to the other side to complete the stretch. This is quite advanced. You can also stand facing a good strong table with the ilium pressed against its edge, bend over to place the torso flat on the table, and perform a back extension from that position.

Question: Do you ever use weights in the exercises you have shown us for additional strengthening?

Answer: Not in the back program. You could do that, but I just don't believe in loading the limbs in extension, especially with dancers, who are so concerned about losing flexibility and "bulking up."

Follow-up Question: I ask because there are some studies now that indicate that proper use of weights can hasten rehabilitation from certain injuries.

Answer: I do use some theraband for ankles. With dancers there is an unwritten rule: five pounds maximum to get a little more work on the vastus medialis. But I would rather just use perfect technique. The problem there has to do with translating what we do in the therapy room to what the dance teacher requires in the studio. Dancers need guidance toward monitoring themselves. Ideally someone would take them through the rigors of their dance class without being rigorous.

Follow-up Comment: Maggie Black, in New York City, is excellent at that.

Answer: Absolutely the best therapy sessions I have had are those at which a knowledgeable dance educator is present. Then we can merge our areas of expertise in dealing with the problems of dancers. Unfortunately, this is seldom practical.

Question: I would like to have your thoughts on the use of theraband in class for strengthening with young dancers.

Answer: I know it has become in vogue to use theraband that way. I still think that if the young dancer is being trained properly to be on the ankle, to work through the pelvis, to be on a very solid base on *relevé*—not to sickle or evert—then ballet technique itself will do the necessary strengthening work. That is what we have always counted on; that is why we go through the prescribed progression of movements on which the ballet class is based. I really think that the proper use of theraband is to restore strength after injury. The image of a bunch of ten year olds using it routinely in conjunction with their ballet classes makes me nervous, as that can easily lead to peroneal tendinitis. I think that weakness at the joints results from poor technique and needs to be addressed by improving the technique.

Question: What particular muscle groups are involved in "snapping hip"?

Answer: That snapping is normally caused by a weakness, or more often an unnecessary holding, at the hip. Where there should be a lengthening of the leg out of the hip socket there is a holding instead, and that causes the tendons to contract. The antidote to that is primarily the floor work where, lying on your back, you do various *rond de jambes*, working always on stabilizing in the pelvis. Snapping is possible at the front of the hip and at the back, but in either case it is almost always a result of having the weight in the legs instead of in the pelvis, where it belongs.

Question: A lot of dancers have severe hyperextension at the knee. Doesn't this cause both anatomical and aesthetic distortions, and how do you deal with it?

Answer: It's true that the more hyperextension you have in the gesturing leg, the stronger you have to be in the pelvis of the supporting leg. When I teach stretching of the leg my main concern is with alignment. I have the dancer sit on the edge of the table, with one leg "in extension" on the table and the other hanging free. Then I check along the length of the extended leg to make sure heel, knee cap and hip socket are aligned (usually if there is a problem it is at the heel). Next I have the dancer bend over the extended leg from the waist, taking hold of the foot and being sure to release in the hip socket. I then try to get her to focus on balancing out the curves at the knee and ankle, maintaining as straight a line as possible at the knee.

Question: What about genu valgum and varum (tibial torsion)?

Answer: Many of the same strategies apply. Again we eliminate weight-bearing by having the dancer sit on the table, this time with both legs extended in front of her. We place a rolled up towel, or something of that sort, under her knees. Then, while we check and encourage her to maintain proper alignment, she levers down to raise the heels off the table. The thing is to consider the desired straightness as originating in the pelvis. This is also the way to deal with all those torsion-producing devices dancers find to add a little something to the line of their turn-out. I discourage any exercise that promotes rotation in any plane other than that which extends out from the pelvis.

Question: Can you talk a little about peroneal tendinitis?

Answer: The important thing is to get dancers to stretch the ankle in, which is an unnatural motion for a ballet dancer. As for strengthening, you have to first achieve reduction of pain and swelling, sometimes just by massaging the tendon, and then you can have the dancer evert her foot against a little resistance. What you are trying to achieve is a full range of pain free motion, and if the dancer can't do *plié-relevé* without pain, then it is too early to start aggressive strengthening exercises. Again, a "quiet hands" type of massage over the affected area is probably the best therapy for this condition— and also the posterior tibialis and flexor hallucis longus— though we also use ice, preferably overnight when the dancer is resting. I am leery of using ice on a hot tendon when the dancer is still active (as during performance), as that numbing can cause her to do something that might increase the severity of the injury.

Question: What about the psychological aspect—the stress—a dancer experiences as a result of having to stay off her legs?

Answer: Yes, that's a genuine concern; if you can't walk on an injured tendon, you obviously can't dance on it. But it doesn't have to be a major issue; these injuries really do clear up if properly managed. I think most dancers get anxious when they have tendinitis, especially the first time, because they think their whole career is in danger. Such anxiety in itself can be conducive to further injury and needs to be dealt with.

Treatment and Rehabilitation of Common Dance Injuries

Christine Ploski, P.T.

What follows is a synopsis of the presentation made by Christine Ploski at the Glasnost Dance Medicine Conference.

I would like to illustrate some of the concepts of physical therapy by describing how we might approach two common dance injuries, patello-femoral stress syndrome and flexor hallucis longus tendinitis.

Simply stated, injuries occur when stress on a bodily structure is greater than the structure can absorb. We generally define two basic types of injury, traumatic and overuse. The two injuries with which I will deal are of the latter sort.

Although they are often considered chronic injuries, overuse injuries do not necessarily have to be chronic. With a thorough physical therapy evaluation, we can identify the problem areas and often teach the patient effective preventative measures.

I am going to concentrate on the anatomic and biomechanical factors involved in dance injuries.

In physical therapy, when we look at a joint like the knee we are particularly concerned with the type and degree of movement present there. We might use a goniometer to measure this. Often with dancers what we find is too much movement at the joint, that the knee is hyperextended. We also look at muscle strength, both static and dynamic, about the joint. Static strength is needed for stability, dynamic strength to produce movement. There are two types of muscle contractions, concentric contractions, which shorten the muscle and generally extend movement, and eccentric contractions, which decelerate and basically control movement. All of these factors must be taken into consideration in planning our therapy program.

In evaluating and treating injuries such as those we will discuss it is especially important to look at postural matters; the degree of internal and external rotation at the hip, for example, can impact heavily on the knee and ankle joints. Injuries often result from muscle imbalance, which in turn relates to postural problems. We need to test carefully for muscle strength and weakness.

Patello-femoral stress syndrome involves abnormal contact between the patellar and the femur. It occurs at all ages, but especially in young dancers. Anything that causes an incongruity between the two surfaces of the patello-femoral joint, be it congenital or developmental, or anything that causes abnormal tracking of the patella, may contribute to this condition. Femoral torsion can also cause knee problems, as can genu-valgum, or knock knee. In dancers, the technical problems that result from trying to force turn-out can definitely be a factor. Overdevelopment of the muscles on the outside of the thigh is a common finding in dancers who experience patello-femoral stress syndrome. We use various tests to detect these problem areas.

The knee joint is particularly vulnerable in dancers, of course, because of the constant demands made on it by the discipline. The same can be said of the flexor hallucis longus tendon. Especially when the dancer goes on *pointe,* or even *demi-pointe,* the tendon has to travel an unusual distance to allow for that movement.

You want to look at the entire foot when dealing with this condition. The diagnostic exercise is to establish a baseline by allowing the dancer to entirely relax the ankle in a nonweight-bearing position and dorsiflex the great toe, then bring the foot up into dorsiflexion (which stretches the tendon tighter) and again dorsiflex the great toe. If one finds a great deal less range of motion this problem should be addressed with flexibility exercises.

[Various exercises used when dealing with these two conditions were demonstrated.]

Strapping for Prevention of Lower Extremity Injuries

Chris Troyanos, A.T.C.

What follows is a synopsis of the presentation made by Chris Troyanos at the Glasnost Dance Medicine Conference.

When dealing with any kind of strapping you first have to ask yourself "What am I trying to accomplish? What are my goals and objectives?" You need to consider whether you are dealing with an acute injury or a chronic problem. What type of motion are you trying to restrict? At what point will the athlete or dancer be allowed to resume activity, and will the strapping be one of the vital keys to getting that person back into training and performance?

In dealing with ankles, the first thing you want to be sure of is that you have a good clean surface. Any dirt will influence the way the tape holds.

There are essentially two types of standard tape: one is a cloth or linen tape with adhesive backing; the other is more elastic, more giving. For the ankle we generally use the former.

Preparation is crucial, so prior to the tape job we want to make sure there are no wounds, cuts, or irritations on any part of the ankle, forefoot, or underneath the foot. Again, the entire area should be clean and clear of any dirt or oils. I have a great deal of trouble with my women's teams, when the members come in after a day in class with lotion on. Under those conditions the tape job will fall down within five min-

45

utes. One thing we do prior to the tape job is to use some type of tape adherent. This is essentially a benzine base with alcohol, which will make the skin tacky. We spray on a good though not excessive coating of that under the foot and around the ankle itself.

When dealing with the ankle there are two main "wear points" that you must take care of, one on the dorsum of the ankle, the other at the base of the Achilles tendon. So we use a little polyethylene foam pad to cover those areas. We have the option of using "underwrap," which is quite elastic and easily applied. I use this on people who are going to be taped frequently—say seven to eight times a week, or even more (as in football). Otherwise, these people can have a good deal of trouble with skin breakdown and irritation. With such people who are participating in team sports, we will often use the underwrap for practices and go directly on the skin for games, as that gives better holding. All of our male athletes are required to shave their ankles. We start with a very light covering of the prewrap on the forefoot and around the ankle, basically "figure eighting" until the entire area is covered.

The kind of strapping I am going to show today is one that the athlete or dancer might wear for general support between performances. We want to position the ankle at 90 degrees, with a slight bit of eversion. Then I like to put one or two anchors slightly below the belly of the gastroc; often the higher you go the better (Figure 1). As what we are trying to do is prevent inversion, the next thing we do is apply three "stirrups," which run from the top of the anchor medially down the ankle, under the forefoot, and up the lateral aspect of the ankle (Figure 2). We fan these forward toward the front of the ankle, so they will lie flat without forming wrinkles in the tape that might cause cuts or blisters (Figures 3-5) and so the base of the stirrups will be wider at the top than at the bottom (where they go under the foot). Then I put a strip around the top of the stirrups, to make sure they stay in place (Figure 6).

I feel you really need a lot of support in the forefoot and arch; the ankle and foot must function together, and without that support you can have problems. So I put in some "J strips." These begin under the foot, come up around the medial aspect of the arch, and run lightly over the ankle and back beyond the posterior edge of the stirrups (Figures 7, 8). These need to be applied lightly because if they are too tight the forefoot won't be able to spread properly in the weight-bearing position. I normally use six of these climbing up the ankle and close them off at top and bottom (Figures 9-12).

The main supportive structures are called "heel locks," and there are several ways to do those. The easiest way is to tear off a strip of tape about 17-18 inches long and hold it at both ends behind the heel, with the sticky side facing you (up). Then you place the tape at an angle you know will work—and this takes time to learn—across the lateral aspect of the heel and wrap one end after the other around and up over the ankle (Figures 13-15). What you have to remember is that tape can give and bend and move slightly. If you happen to miss your angle the first time, the tape is easily taken off and you can start again. I then run six to eight "closure strips" up the leg to hold everything in place, and that completes the basic part of the job (Figures 16-21).

This strapping should allow for a reasonable amount of plantar flexion, but when the dancer stands and tries to roll to the lateral aspect she should feel that the ankle is being held in place.

Question: What is the general hold rate on this versus some sort of compression or air-cast?

Answer: This goes back again to what you are trying to accomplish. I like air-casts, but more for the treatment of acute ankle sprains than as a supportive measure in dance or athletics. What happens with an air-cast in a sneaker, with a sock, is that you get too much slippage. Better than that, in my opinion, is something called a "lace-up sock," which comes in many varieties. This allows for more stability in the shoe and doesn't do so much damage to the shoe itself. But in all honesty, I am most partial to the tape.

Question: What about the expense involved?

Answer: The average taping costs about $1.50. By the way, once you know what you are doing, a tape job of this sort shouldn't take more than a minute.

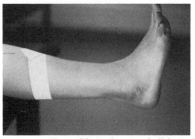

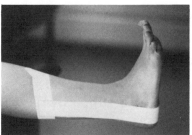

Figure 1: The ankle is clean and all hair is removed by shaving. Tape adherent is sprayed on. The first strip applied is an "anchor." This strip is placed at the muscular tendon junction of the gastrocnemius. The tape must be angled slightly, to allow it to conform smoothly to the shape of the leg.

Figure 2: The first of three "stirrups" is applied. These strips of tape start on the medial aspect of the lower leg, continue down, over and behind the medial malleolus, under the foot and arch, then up the lateral aspect of the foot to the upper anchor. Pressure is always applied laterally as the calcaneus and the talus are pulled into a neutral position. This strip should cover the back half of the medial and lateral malleoli.

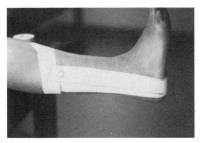

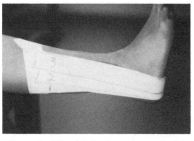

Figure 3: The second stirrup is applied. This should cover one-half of the first stirrup.

Figure 4: The third stirrup is applied in the same way as the second, but it is slightly angled to avert impingement at the base of the fifth metatarsal.

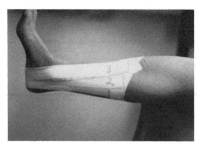

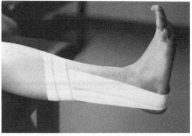

Figure 5: Medial view.

Figure 6: A second anchor is applied to hold the stirrups in place.

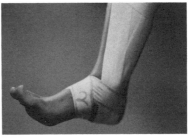

Figure 7: The first of six "J" supports is applied to the forefoot. These strips of tape are used for arch/forefoot stability and support.

Figure 8: The second "J" support is in place. Note the "X" that is created over the dorsum of the foot. These strips of tape should be placed with a minimum amount of tension, so as not to constrict the forefoot.

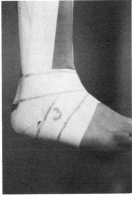

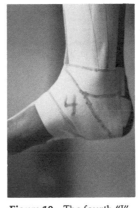

Figure 9: The third "J" support is in place. Note that each support is overlapping the original by one-half, as it is being placed proximal to the last strip (lateral view).

Figure 10: The fourth "J" support is in place (medial view)

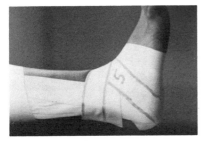

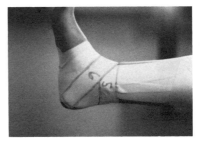

Figure 11: The fifth "J" support is in place (lateral view).

Figure 12: The sixth "J" support is in place (medial view).

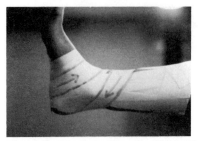

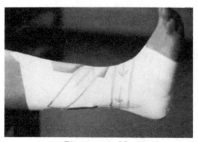

Figure 13: The first of four "heel locks" is applied (medial view). These supports are designed to prevent sub-talar movement for both inversion and eversion. A heel lock is applied by starting on the top of the instep and then taking the tape under the foot, behind the heel, and around the leg. Heel locks should be applied in both directions.

Figure 14:   Heel lock (lateral view).

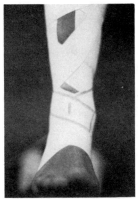

Figure 15:   Heel lock (lateral view).

Figure 16:   The first of six to eight "closures" is applied. These strips of tape complete the strapping and hold the stirrups and heel locks in place.

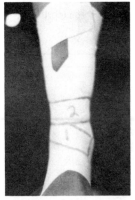

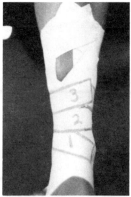

Figure 17:   Again, the second and successive layers should cover the original strip of tape by one-half.

Figure 18:   The third closure strip in place.

Figure 19: Completion of preventive ankle strapping.

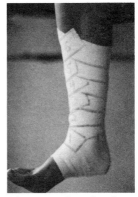

Figure 20: Completed ankle strapping (medial view).

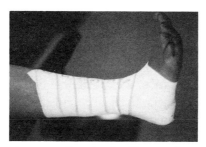

Figure 21: Completed ankle strapping (lateral view).

The Psychological Aspects of Dance and the Dancer

Linda Hamilton, Ph.D.

What follows is a synopsis of the paper presented by Linda Hamilton at the Glasnost Dance Medicine Conference.

This presentation will concentrate on three issues that are pertinent to a ballet dancer's experience: First, I will discuss the psychological aspects; then, some of the consequences of engaging in such a demanding but short career; and last, suggestions for services to help mitigate some of the problems involved.

A professional ballet career usually begins in the late teens. Most dancers come to the home city where their new company resides from other states and sometimes other countries. They leave their parents at a very young age to enter their company's ballet school. Their identity as a dancer forms at this time as they increasingly choose ballet over peer relationships, dating, and higher education. Marriage is often postponed, since there is little time or energy left over after a twelve hour work day. As the ballet company comes to represent the only security the dancer knows, aging during middle adulthood and any significant injury can easily take on the form of a major life crisis.

The overall message for the professional dancer is to be young, healthy, and thin. This is particularly true for females, who must conform to an ideal body weight considerably below the norm. Unfortunately, maintaining a low weight is difficult since ballet dancing does not share the high energy expenditure of many athletic endeavors. Typically the female ballet dancer expends only 200 calories in a one hour ballet class.

In order to see in what ways a professional dancer's diet might reflect her concern with maintaining a low weight, we conducted a 24-hour nutritional survey on 19 dancers from the New York City Ballet and American Ballet Theater. The findings reveal that, on the whole, dancers tend to be undernourished when compared to control women of similar age, weight, and height. More than one half of the dancers were consuming less than 85% of the recommended daily allowance of calories in spite of the fact that they were dancing three to four hours a day. Their diets were also low in nutritional density, with the majority taking in less than the RDA for calcium, iron, and niacin. Furthermore, weight concerns were found to be directly related to how and what the dancers were eating. Dancers who were terrified of being fat had diets with significantly less fat, protein, niacin, and iron than those without this concern.

Besides poor nutrition, dancers are also at risk for the development of eating problems. In a study by Garner and Garfinkel, dance students were found to have a seven-fold increased chance of developing anorexia nervosa in comparison with their high school counterparts. Interestingly, this was directly related to the level of competition of the different ballet schools. Dancers from more competitive settings had double the incidence of anorexia nervosa—7.6% as compared to 3.5% in dancers from less competitive settings.

These findings led us to speculate on the incidence of eating problems within the competitive setting of the ballet company. We surveyed 55 female dancers in four regional and national companies in America. It was expected that the incidence of anorexia nervosa would be higher in national companies, where the requirements for entry and promotion are more stringent. The results supported this hypothesis; 22% of the national dancers were found to have anorexia nervosa. No incidence was reported in regional dancers. The national dancers also stated that their companies' standard for thinness was significantly more rigid than that of the regional dancers, and they were required to diet more.

Following up these findings, we asked why some dancers developed serious eating problems while others did not. We looked for the answer in the research on dieting. Recent studies suggest that a genetic setpoint for weight exists, which determines the amount of fat stored in the body by regulating perceptions of hunger, activity level, and metabolic rate. Family-line resemblances in fatness can run as high as 80%, and are present across the whole range of body fatness—from very thin to very fat. As a result, going on a diet can be seen as an attempt to overpower the body's natural level of fatness by resisting its setpoint. Restrained eaters would then face certain inevitable hazards, as this comprises a counter-regulatory behavior, accompanied by severe psychological distress.

In line with this theory, we hypothesized that dancers who were not naturally thin would be more vulnerable to the development of serious eating problems. To investigate this hypothesis, we examined the incidence of familial obesity and eating problems in the dancers of two national companies from vastly different cultures, American and Mainland China. These companies share the same stringent process of early recruitment and selection from their own schools. The Chinese dancers also have the same Russian training and emphasis on thinness as American dancers. It was expected that dancers from different cultures, who had been selected in this manner, would show similar and relatively low incidences of eating problems and familial obesity. We also compared the American company with two additional American companies which, while from the same culture, choose their dancers from auditions. Differences were expected from these groups, since national companies that hold open auditions would not have exercised control over the early selection process of their dancers.

Five percent of the highly selected Americans and 12% of the Chinese dancers reported a close family member to be obese. In the American sample, 42% of the dancers from open auditions had an obese family member. When the incidence of eating problems was examined for the two groups, no significant differences were found between the highly selected dancers, with 11% of the Americans and 24% of the Chinese reporting either anorexia, bulimia, or purging behavior.

Significant differences were found among the American dancers: 46% of the less selected Americans reporting eating problems as compared to 11% of the highly selected dancers. The less selected dancers also reported significantly more anorexic behaviors than the highly selected Americans.

These findings suggest that national ballet companies that do not control the early selection process of their dancers may be choosing women who have more difficulty maintaining the low weight demanded by this profession. Further, it would seem that the less selected dancers may be achieving an appropriately low weight by practicing deviant eating behaviors. The fact that these dancers reported significantly more eating problems and anorexic behaviors than the highly selected dancers lends support for this thesis.

Obviously, the consequences of achieving a low weight may be profound if you are not naturally thin. However, the aesthetic component is only one stressful factor in classical ballet. There is also the need to be healthy and young enough to perform. In order to better understand the impact of injuries and the prospect of retirement on their lives, we surveyed 35 female dancers, who were currently performing in two major national ballet companies in America. Questionnaires were distributed that addressed the dancer's injury history, their thoughts about retirement, alcohol and drug use, and mental status. An analysis of the results revealed that over two thirds of the group had sustained a major dance injury . Fifty percent were also seriously contemplating retirement. When dancers with and without injuries were compared, significant differences were found in both lifestyles and psychological equilibrium. Injured dancers were found to use both drugs and alcohol more than dancers who did not have physical problems; 38% reported that they had considered suicide. In the uninjured dancers, no incidence of suicidal ideation was found.

Regarding retirement, older dancers were found to consider this possibility significantly more than younger dancers, with age being given as the most common reason for leaving this career. The projected age of departure for this group was 34. Few of the dancers had any specific plans for the future. The prospect of retirement was significantly related to impaired psychological functioning. Women who were contemplating retirement used a higher proportion of drugs; they also reported significantly more suicidal ideation.

The results of this study suggest that, for individuals who have spent a lifetime working at something they love, forced retirement can be a dreaded event. Far from being a new beginning, it may merely usher in a series of losses that encompass income, workplace, community, and most important, loss of identity.

In general, ballet dancers tend to become isolated from people and interests outside their profession. There is a tendency to interact only with other dancers in the same company. This one-dimensional way of life often extends beyond their social relationships to encompass shared social and political values, and may interfere with the development of other capacities. As a result, few dancers have resources or training to fall back on outside of their art form. Faced with the realities of retirement, aging or injured performers are at a distinct disadvantage. Not only is their support system gone, but they may be on their own for the first time, without being adequately prepared to assume a meaningful role in society.

Given the various consequences of pursuing a life in classical ballet, it seems relevant to consider what services might help to alleviate or prevent some of these problems. Nutritional counseling and education about appropriate dieting techniques would appear to be important. It might also be necessary to pay greater attention to selection factors. Women who are not naturally thin and have trouble keeping their weight down might better be counseled to choose an athletic discipline where the caloric expenditure is higher and a thin body is not a requirement. For those who are injured, adequate time must be allowed for recovery; the healing time could be used constructively to reevaluate work habits that might have led to the injury in the first place. Finally, for those who are having difficulty leaving this career, vocational counseling and support groups would be useful.

While dancers do come from a sheltered environment, they have extraordinary self-discipline and an ability to work under pressure that can readily transfer to a diverse range of occupations outside of dance. Dance medicine professionals who are aware of the special needs of these individuals have the opportunity to help them cope with and eventually move beyond the narrow, although exhilarating, world of the performing arts to utilize other aspects of their evolving personalities.

Dancers in Transition

Ellen Wallach

What follows is a synopsis of the presentation made by Ellen Wallach at the Glasnost Dance Medicine Conference.

If you are currently dancing and have set an imaginary end-date on your performing career, research indicates that you will actually stop five years before that.

Fifty-one percent of female modern dancers report never having thought of retirement.

Few former dancers report knowing a year before their retirement that the end was that near.

My research was done with former dancers, which created a problem right from the beginning: How do you locate former dancers? Typically we find, especially in ballet, that when dancers retire they are cut out of the company family, and left entirely to their own devices. Hence, they tend to disappear. I ended up with over 800 names and addresses, to which I sent my eight-page questionnaire. I received 300 responses, which is an amazing return. I must point out, however, that even this 40% rate of return skews my results; I heard only from those ex-dancers who were willing to discuss their experiences after dance. The rest have "fallen in a crack."

I found that 68% of the people who leave dance stay in a dance-related profession; 42% of the female ballet dancers teach; 42% of the male ballet dancers are artistic directors or administrators. This gender bias does not hold true in the modern dance world: 24% of the male and female modern

dancers are administrators and artistic directors and 14% are
university professors.

There is a very large career-transitions-in-dance project in
Canada, headed by former New York City ballet dancer
Joysanne Sidimus. When she asked dancers who were currently dancing in 1985 how many of them expected to teach,
only 13% answered affirmatively. In my study I found that
41% do. One thing we are trying to do is find options for
these people who are working at jobs they appear not to have
chosen.

When I asked my subjects whether they would choose to
dance again, 89% said they would, including 95% of the male
ballet dancers. The lowest percentage was the female modern
dancers (82%). Overall, 94% said they were satisfied with
their careers.

So why do people quit? Some are "pushed"—by injury,
age, lack of work, burn-out, etc. Others are "pulled," by new
job offers, the desire to do something else in a new way, etc.
Generally, men get pulled, and women get pushed.

The better one is prepared for life after dance, the easier
the transition. Typically, dancers are least prepared finan-
cially: 88% experience some emotional or physical problem;
61% said they had an identity crisis.

Transition tends to be marked by recognizable stages: first
denial, then anger, bargaining, depression, and finally accep-
tance. These stages are not necessarily linear—the order might
change, some might be delayed, they might overlap—but
overall they add up to a process of grieving.

When my information is compared with that provided by
the Canadian study of current dancers mentioned above, and
another conducted by PACH in 1983 in New York City, the
picture is not as bleak as one might expect. What dancers find
in retirement tends not to be as bad as they think it is going to
be. The problem with getting dancers to think about transition
is that they are so frightened; they don't want to look at it.

The principal message where transition is concerned is
prepare, prepare, prepare. Female ballet dancers tend to be
the least prepared, and therefore experience transition as a
sudden and unexpected change. Yet, dancers are survivors.
What I found is that 78% had a new committed activity after

one year, 90% after two years. The truth of the matter is that dance is excellent training for work in the "real" world.

Where do dancers find emotional support after retirement? As already suggested, they get it least from dance management and artistic staff. Shockingly, there is also less support from family and friends than dancers expect. This is often their biggest disappointment.

The first message I try to give to people is that you are not a dancer; you are a person who dances, and when you stop dancing you will still be a person. The real issue is not what dancers do, but the psychological readiness to do it.

Among things that are happening in this area, some of those most worthy of mention are: Beyond Dance, sponsored by the entire dance community of Seattle; the Transition Center of AGMA; and the established and successful Dancer Transition Centre in Canada. The Western Europeans tend to have government sponsored retirement programs, so they do not have the extreme problems we do.

Questions and Answers

Question: It has been observed that there tend to be "five-year shifts" in the way performing artists perceive their careers. Do you have any plans to study such shifts longitudinally?

Answer: I have never done a longitudinal study, and I suspect it will never be done. There is no funding for that kind of effort.

Question/Statement: I am from Western Europe, and I don't believe your observation about State support for dance in those countries is accurate. As far as I know, virtually all Western European dance companies are privately funded.

Answer: I don't know it firsthand, but I have been told that there are schemes in Great Britain, Germany, Holland and the Scandinavian countries for state support.

Reply from the floor: I think things are as bad in those countries as here. Holland is the best. Until recently dance has not been considered as a real profession, so the schemes for public funding have not applied.

Question: Are current dancers willing to talk about their retirement plans?

Answer: It's really a Catch-22; you offer a workshop on transitions for current dancers and nobody shows up because they are too busy. So the artistic director says "We offered a program and nobody was interested, so let's not go any further with this." I think it is true that current performers want to avoid this subject.

Question: Did you find that the difference in educational level between modern and ballet dancers influences the kinds of occupations they consider in transition?

Answer: I can tell you statistically that the difference in level does exist; approximately 60% of all modern dancers have a college degree or more, while about the same percentage of ballet dancers have a high school degree or less. However, the kind of correlation you are asking about is hard to determine. It is very clear that female modern dancers have the hardest time during transition—and are the best educated.

Anatomy as a Master Image in Training Dancers

Professor Ruth Solomon

What follows is an article reprinted with permission from the Journal of Physical Education, Recreation and Dance, May/June, 1987, pp. 51-56. It is offered as a summation of Professor Solomon's video presentation and workshop at the Glasnost Dance Medicine Conference. The Journal is a publication of the American Alliance for Health, Physical Education, Recreation and Dance, 1900 Association Drive, Reston, VA 22091.

The most basic principle on which my approach to training dancers rests is that the impetus for all movement originates deep within the dancer's body, that movement is propelled out from "the center," through the body, into space. The second tenet is that although this fact may have psychological and even metaphysical implications (which I will not address here), and definitely <u>does</u> influence the aesthetics of dance, in the studio it is best dealt with on a strictly physical level. Hence, my career as a dancer/teacher has been closely tied to the search for a language, or better yet a set of visual images, to describe what is happening in the body as it moves.

Not surprisingly, the most precise, intelligible, and comprehensive imagery—and language—I have found is that provided by anatomy, exactly as that science has been developed, studied, and utilized by the medical profession. I use anatomical terms and images with students to describe the mechanics of movement. My class is structured to involve the student immediately not only in "warming up," but in identifying (making contact with), isolating, aligning, and strengthening the most essential body parts. All the exercises with which my warm-up begins have to do with imaging the flow of motion through the <u>bones</u>. Incidentally, we concern ourselves with the muscles that control this system—especially the psoas.

There is one other general facet of my approach to teaching that requires a few words before turning to some specific exercises. Throughout the warm-up I use vocalization as an integral part of virtually every exercise; that is, I ask the students to make sounds—more than just breathing sounds; actual words or vocalized syllables—on the strong effort aspect of each movement. Thus, an audible breath/sound pattern is created; allow the breath in on the release aspect of the movement, breathe (sound) out on the strong effort.

Because of space limitations I will describe only the exercises with which my warm-up begins, but in explaining how and why I do these exercises I should be able to illustrate some of the principles on which this approach to training dancers is based. It is important to note that although for the sake of clarity I am describing individual exercises here, in reality these exercises constitute a sequence, one flowing developmentally into another without pause.

Standing relaxed, with the feet in parallel position, arms above the head (Figure 1a), curve the lumbar spine back, keeping the shoulders over the hip sockets and bending the knees as needed to deepen the curve (Figure 1b). This articulation in the lumbar area allows the spine, from lumbar through sacrum and coccyx, to form one continuous curve, the lower end of which, if extended forward in imagination between the legs, would strike the floor at a point well in front of the feet. We are aided in this imaging by the curve of the coccyx which, when viewed in profile, already tilts forward. The lumbar articulation simply deepens and extends that curve. By keeping the shoulders over the hip sockets we cause the dorsal spine to reflect the curve below it; hence, the entire spine, up through the cervical curve, is drawn into one continuous arc. Enhancing the dorsal curve has the additional advantage of releasing the rib cage—indeed, the dorsal spine can't curve if the rib cage is held forward or lifted—in turn relieving tension in the psoas, which is being pulled in the opposite direction to create the lumbar curve.

This effort cycle of the exercise is given three counts, and sounded with one continuous word—exhalation, for example "oouut." Then release for three counts, allowing the breath in and returning to the standing position, again making sure that the shoulders remain over the hip sockets (Figure 1c). This simple exercise allows us to focus our attention on the center-of-movement area, to articulate virtually the whole spine in relation to that center, thus beginning to warm it up and align it, and to engage the psoas directly in this process.

Once you have done enough repetitions of this exercise to sense the area in which you are working, move on to exercise two. This begins with the same standing lumbar curve (Figure 2a), which is maintained and lowered by bending the knees until the coccyx almost touches the floor (Figure 2b). Hang in this position for three counts, and then roll backward on the curve, keeping the knees close into the chest to deepen it, touch the floor behind the head with the toes (three counts, Figure 2c), and roll forward on the curve until you are back on your feet (three counts, Figure 2d). It is important that the feet, knees, and thighs remain in parallel, and the knees should be over the second toe. Again hang in this low parallel position for three counts, and then rise to standing (three counts), as always making sure that the shoulders are over the hip sockets (Figure 2e). This exercise continues using the same movement sequence with a more rapid continuous flow of motion, completing the exercise in six counts; three counts for rolling down until toes touch the floor behind the head, and three counts for rolling forward to stand. The use of the lumbar curve in this exercise—first establishing it, then controlling with it as the body's weight is lowered to the floor, then rolling on it (which we could not do smoothly if the spine were not consistently curved)—provides ample opportunity to experience and thereby image the spine.

End exercise two by releasing the spine flat onto the floor instead of completing the forward roll in the last repetition and, with bent knees, allowing the feet to land flat in parallel (Figure 3a). This places you in position to begin exercise three, which involves what I call "pelvic rocks." First roll the lower spine off the floor, starting with the coccyx and continuing as far as the 12th dorsal vertebra (Figure 3b). This I call an

Figure 1a   Figure 1b   Figure 1c

Figure 2a   Figure 2b

Figure 2c   Figure 2d   Figure 2e

Figure 3a

Figure 3b

Figure 3c

Figure 4a

Figure 4b

Figure 4c

Figure 4d

"undercurve"—the equivalent of the "pelvic tilt" in many other techniques (and much physical therapy). The "rock" is completed by reversing this process into an "overcurve" (Figure 3c), which requires a release of the hip socket (rectus femoris and iliacus). This exercise is performed first on two slow counts, then the time is doubled, and doubled again.

Exercise four develops on three in much the same way two did on one. Starting in the same position, and having established the same undercurve from coccyx through sacrum to 12th dorsal (Figure 4a), extend the undercurve up the spine until resting on the shoulder blades, thus fully involving the dorsal spine in the articulation (Figure 4b). Then start down from the top, cascading the entire spine onto the floor (Figure 4c), and ending in an overcurve (Figure 4d). The breathing is especially important in this exercise and the one that follows, as students tend to hold their breath through the strong effort cycles. The movement is designed to combat this tendency; we breathe/sound out for four counts as the pelvis rises, release and allow air in for two counts at the top, breathe/sound out for four counts coming down, and release for air in for two counts in the overcurve.

Exercise five maintains this same breathing pattern and begins in the same way, but having released for two counts at the top (Figure 5a), reverse the downward flow of the vertebrae by lowering the coccyx to the floor first (Figure 5b), then the sacrum and dorsal spine (Figure 5c).

As a relief from our focus on the spine, and in order to get some blood flowing through the limbs and joints, exercise six focuses on the legs and arms. Exercise five has left you with spine and feet flat on the floor, knees bent. Now lift the legs and shake them loosely for eight counts, letting air in (Figure 6a). Then flex the feet, bend the knees slightly, and, holding that basic shape, vibrate the legs vigorously, sounding the breath out for eight counts (Figure 6b). Then drop the feet heavily onto the floor in parallel position and repeat essentially the same process with the arms, first shaking them loosely (Figure 6c), then shaping them at the elbows and wrists and vibrating for eight counts (Figure 6d).

Exercises seven and eight begin as we lift our bent legs above us, knees softly folded, and take hold of the tibias with

Figure 5a

Figure 5b

Figure 5c

Figure 6a

Figure 6b

Figure 6c

Figure 6d

our hands (Figure 7a). Then, by pressing through the knees into the hands, drag the head off the floor (Figure 7b), and, breathing/sounding out, let it curve sequentially forward (Figure 7c). This simple movement articulates the dorsal and cervical vertebrae, the ones that have been only marginally worked earlier. Then release the spine back onto the floor, allowing the air in, and repeat. Gradually begin to rock on the lumbar curve (Figure 8a), rounding it down to a base of support in the sacrum, and "lever" down through this base of support to bring yourself onto a balance point slightly behind the coccyx (Figure 8b). The exact placement differs from one individual to another. The levering action—pressing down to rise—is one of those keys to motion that is easily visualized and experienced through the anatomical approach. Even when we are up on the balance point, the lumbar and dorsal spine remains in an easy curve. It is important not to try to straighten the spine entirely because to do so causes undue strain on the low back, which must then support the weight of the legs. Breathe/sound out on the levering (effort) action, and release for air in as the body curves back down to the starting position.

All the final exercises in this sequence begin on the balance point. In exercise nine circle the head, first to the side (Figure 9a), then forward (Figure 9b), then side (Figure 9c), and back (Figure 9d), sounding out on the extension back, which is the long arc of the cervical vertebrae. Reverse direction each time to make sure the vertebrae are being articulated equally on all sides. It is important throughout this exercise to maintain an open throat, for easy passage of breath and voice.

In exercise ten rotate the arms from the shoulders, first one at a time (Figures 10a and b), then both together, back to front, then reversing the circle (Figures 10c, d, and e). This not only lubricates the shoulder joints, but has the added advantage of causing the psoas, which is already engaged in sustaining the body on the balance point, to work even harder to offset the free flow of the arms. The same effect is heightened in exercise 11, where the extension of the legs is added to the work the psoas is doing, extending them in a V shape with the torso, femurs as close to the chest as possible, and tibias articulated to line up with femurs (Figure 11a). Then alternately fold at

Figure 7a

Figure 7b

Figure 7c

Figure 8a

Figure 8b

Figure 9a

Figure 9b

Figure 9c

Figure 9d

Figure 10a

Figure 10b

Figure 10c

Figure 10d

Figure 10e

Figure 11a

Figure 11b

Figure 12a

Figure 12b

Figure 12c

Figure 12d

Figure 12e

Figure 12f

the knees (Figure 11b) and straighten the legs, breathing/ sounding out as the tibias extend and releasing for breath in as they fold. This exercise also starts to lubricate the knee joints.

Exercise 12 works primarily on lubricating and warming up the hip joints (and strengthening the psoas). From the starting position on the balance point, knees together in parallel and arms extended outside the legs (Figure 12a), open the knees to the side, bringing the arms inside the legs (Figure 12b). Then reverse the process—knees in, arms out (Figure 12c). After each set of four repetitions catch the ankles and allow the weight of the legs to rest in the palms of the hands, releasing the hip sockets.

Having performed this exercise several times with bent knees, straighten the legs and continue, thus increasing the need for control in the pelvis (Figures 12d, e, and f). It should be clear that the strength and facility we are developing throughout these balance-point exercises is exactly what we will use when, in standing position, we work on extension.

The final exercises in this sequence complete the first phase in preparing for standing work. In exercise 13, still on the balance point with the legs out straight in a raised second position, take hold of the ankles and fold the knees in (Figure 13a), then return to extended legs in second (Figure 13b). As always, breathe/sound out on the extension, in on the release.

In exercise 14, with the legs together and extended in parallel, alternately flex and point the feet (Figures 14a and b). This begins to warm up the ankles and feet. Lastly, let go with the hands and, while continuing to flex and point the feet and maintaining the lumbar-dorsal curve, lower the legs until the heels are six to eight inches off the floor (Figures 15a and b). Then, with the feet flexed, rotate the legs out from the hip sockets, and cross or "beat" the legs as in *entrechat* for at least four sets of eight (Figure 15c). Finally, lowering the legs flat onto the floor, lever down through the sacrum, bringing the torso up to sitting position, and then, releasing in the hip sockets, allow the torso to fold over the legs (Figure 15d). It is important in this final phase to make sure that all the muscles around the hip socket—the tensor fascia lata, rectus femoris, and iliacus—are released. The principle throughout exercises 11 to 15 is to articulate the lower leg while maintaining a soft

Figure 13a

Figure 13b

Figure 14a

Figure 14b

Figure 15a

Figure 15b

Figure 15c

Figure 15d

hip socket and <u>not</u> engaging the quadriceps as the primary motivator of the movements.

This entire sequence takes approximately ten minutes when each exercise is repeated four to six times.

In my view it is the main business of dance technique classes to eliminate the tendencies that lead to inefficient and deleterious movement and get the students working in a more effective manner. We can do this by using the language and imagery of anatomy to explain exactly how movement comes about. I emphasize the roles of the psoas, the pelvis, and the spine because the study of anatomy has led me to believe that they are the prime motivators of movement. If the dancer is able to visualize and thereby control these components in action all else should follow, and the movement produced will be relatively stress-free and efficient.

Research in Prevention of Dance Injury

Priscilla Clarkson, Ph.D.

What follows is a synopsis of the presentation made by Priscilla Clarkson at the Glasnost Dance Medicine Conference.

Along with my colleagues Andrea Watkins at the University of Massachusetts and Ann McNeal from Hampshire College I have been examining several factors related to dance injury. The first factor we considered was turn-out.[1]

Our research plan was to develop a method by which any dance teacher could assess turn-out and determine if a dancer was forcing turn-out. We had our dancer-subjects stand on a large piece of paper, on which we traced their feet. Then we dropped a plumb-line from the tibial tuberosity to where it touched the paper when the dancer did a *plié* in first position, in left fifth, and right fifth. We determined the mid-heel and mid-forefoot points, and connected those to create our "reference line." The angle between the reference lines of the two feet formed the measurement of turn-out. The point at which the plumb-line from the knee hit the paper marked the deviation from the reference line. By drawing a line through the deviation point we could calculate the angle of deviation. The more closely the knee fell over the foot, the smaller the angle of deviation would be.

We sampled 350 dancers. Of these, 22 were young dancers, age 10 to 13. There were 171 pre-professional dancers, at least 13 years of age and performing with a local company, and 58 were college dancers enrolled in an advanced college ballet class. Finally, there were 99 professional ballet dancers, 15 of whom were male. We recorded the time each subject spent in class, rehearsal and performance, and understandably this measurement reflected their commitment to the art form. Generally, the young dancers and the pre-professionals were found to be spending about 25 hours per week dancing.

No one in our sampling had 180 degrees of turn-out; one rare dancer had 175 degrees. The young dancers as a group had the largest degree of turn-out, the college dancers the smallest. The pre-professionals and professionals, in the middle, were very similar.

With regard to the degree of deviation, no one had zero deviation—i.e., the knee directly over the second toe in turned-out position. The college dancers, who had the least turn-out, also had the least deviation; the young dancers, with the greatest degree of turn-out, also had the largest degree of deviation—i.e., their knees were falling farthest toward the center. This strongly suggests that the young dancers were forcing their turn-out.

We next correlated deviation with self-reported injury history. We found, again understandably, that the number of injuries generally followed the number of years dancing (the longer you dance the more likely you are to experience injury). An exception, however, was seen in foot and ankle injuries to young dancers, which were surprisingly prevalent. This may support the thesis that forced turn-out causes injuries, though none of the groups showed a direct correlation between angle of deviation and incidence of injury at any potential injury site. We think this points to a weakness in cross sectional studies (like ours). A more accurate way to study a problem like the one we set ourselves here might be to follow a group of subjects longitudinally, that is, over a longer time span.

In another study we looked at pronation, which most people in the dance medicine field believe is a condition that is conducive to injury.[2] Many dance teachers report frustration in trying to correct this condition in their students.

Working with Dr. Robert James at the University of Massachusetts, we experimented with what is basically a biofeedback technique. We strapped a small transducer under the arch of the subject's foot. This was connected to an amplifier and an earphone, through which the dancer received a "buzz" each time she pronated enough to engage the transducer. By way of another connection each incidence of pronation was also graphed on a pen recorder, so we could measure the frequency and extent of pronation.

Over the course of three days each subject performed four "bouts" of movement, each bout being composed of various *tendus* and *frappés*. For some bouts one group of dancers received no feedback; during others a dance teacher standing nearby told them repeatedly to "pull up your ankles." The other group of dancers received the electronic "buzz" feedback. In the first two cases there was minimal improvement toward eliminating the pronation on the first day, which tended to dissipate over time. With the feedback technique there was immediate progress to zero pronation, which tended to hold for the duration of testing. This appears to be a very successful technique, with which we have had good results both in the laboratory and in the studio.

Our principal concern is to reduce injuries, especially in young dancers. Through experimentation of the sort on which I have reported we, and others like us, hope to achieve that goal.

Questions and Answers

Question: With regard to the turn-out study, couldn't there be other operative causes of injury?

Answer: You are right, there could be many causes. This was our initial attempt to examine what is happening in a large group of dancers.

Question: Is what the dancers did when you were measuring their turn-out necessarily what they do when they are dancing?

Answer: It is probably at least close to what they do at the *barre*. I agree with the thrust of your question, though. It would be far better to have a videotape system from which you could do motion analysis. You could probably do these same measurements from a film analysis.

Question: Did you look at turn-out through the growth spurt?

Answer: No, we looked at it one time only. I think one of the interesting findings, though, is that these young dancers, the 10 to 11 year olds, seem able to force turn-out very easily, and I believe dance teachers should know that.

Question: Did you standardize how the *plié* was performed? Was the turn-out established in knee flexion or extension?

Answer: Dancers were asked to perform a *demi plié* that they would typically do at the *barre*. The turn-out was established in knee extension (standing), and once the feet were set in position (and traced on the paper) they couldn't be moved.

Question: How did you find your mid-foot point?

Answer: That was a set measurement of 40 millimeters from the back of the heel.

Question: Would you hypothesize that the basically static biofeedback results would carry over to dynamic work?

Answer: Yes, judging from what we know about similar work in sports. That would be an interesting follow-up experiment, to see if the dancers were able to retain the corrections we observed.

Question: Was any effort made to look at the sources of pronation?

Answer: No, though I agree that there can be various sources.

Question: There are at least two ways to interpret your findings regarding forced turn-out in young dancers: On the one hand, we might view that as a viable way of increasing turn-out; on the other, we might see it only as a potential source of injury. What are your thoughts?

Answer: We have found that many of the young dancers who are forcing turn-out because they believe that is the thing to do have pain in their knees; they are not necessarily injured, but their knees hurt. I believe that forcing turn-out at the knee, as opposed to turning out from the hips, can cause serious problems over time.

References

1. Watkins A., Woodhull-McNeal A.P., Clarkson, P.M., and Ebbeling C. Lower extremity alignment and injury in young, pre-professional, college, and professional ballet dancers: Part 1. Turnout and knee-foot alignment. *Medical Problems of Performing Artists* 4:148-153, 1989.

2. Clarkson P.M., James R.J., Watkins A., and Foley P. The effect of augmented feedback on foot pronation during *barre* exercise in dance. *Research Quarterly for Sport and Exercise* 57:33-40, 1986.

A Prospective Study of Physiological Characteristics of Ballet Dancers

Daniel S. Rooks, Sc.D.

What follows is a synopsis of the presentation made by Daniel S. Rooks at the Glasnost Dance Medicine Conference.

The factors that we address in considering injury prevention within the context of dance, or sports medicine in general, can be classified as either intrinsic variables, which deal specifically with the anatomical, physiological, and psychosocial factors that make up an individual, or extrinsic variables, which include footwear, performance surface, ambient temperature, etc. The majority of injury prevention work to date has primarily examined extrinsic factors.

Another set of terms for describing research in this field is retrospective vs. prospective assessment. Retrospective evaluation examines the relationship variables have to each other after data have been gathered. Prospective method means working step-by-step in a longitudinal fashion, taking measurements, keeping injury histories, and correlating the data in an on-going manner. Today I would like to introduce you to a study we in the Division of Sports Medicine at Children's Hospital have started. We are looking at the role of intrinsic variables in young dancers. Our method of study will be prospective.

The questions we are asking are as follows:

1. What physiological characteristics are needed to be a successful dancer? This question obviously has been asked many times—including by our Russian guests—and we hope

to be able to identify factors that will contribute to answering it.

2. What intrinsic characteristics may place a child at risk for musculo-skeletal injury? We are looking for specific anatomical, physiological, or psychological factors that place a child at risk for injury in the short term. Also, we are looking for factors that, over the course of five years, may bring about adverse changes.

3. How does habitual training in ballet counteract the physical changes that occur with normal growth? Obviously we will be looking mainly at the adverse changes that predispose a child to injury.

Our subjects are 8-9 year old children who are training regularly at the Boston Ballet School. It is advantageous to our study that these students will receive their training under similar conditions. Our control group of nondancers will be drawn from local public and private schools. The methods of the study will include a complete history, including medical and injury information. Of particular interest is the family history back through the grandparent generation. We are assessing dietary history and looking at psychological profiles of the young dancers. Each child undergoes a medical examination and orthopaedic assessment. Musculo-skeletal characteristics are assessed through anthropometric evaluation, strength, flexibility, and cardiovascular testing. I hope to be able to see you all in five years to report on our findings!

Questions and Answers

Question: Is femoral anteversion really such a bad thing in children who want to do ballet?

Answer: It is that kind of information that we lack at present and will be exploring through our study. Although we have heard some cautionary notes about that condition at this conference, I don't think anyone who has spoken to you here would rule out participation for the child who is involved in dance for the sheer enjoyment of physical activity, learning, and being with her friends.

Question: Will your control group be doing any kind of physical training?

Answer: Yes, we are not going to restrict their activities.

Question: What about the fact that some of your subjects will be weeded out during the course of your study?

Answer: I would prefer not to use the term "weeded out." True, some subjects will drop out, but that kind of attrition is expected in any longitudinal study. For that reason we try to start with as large a subject population as possible.

3

ROUNDTABLE DISCUSSION

Roundtable Discussion: The Dancer and Injury

Lyle J. Micheli, M.D.,
Moderator

What follows are synopses of brief statements offered by each participant.

Role of the Artistic Director and Choreographer, *Bruce Marks*

The dance career is subject to many pitfalls. My own career began in 1950 at the High School of Performing Arts in New York City. I knew virtually nothing about dance when I went there; I had been tap dancing above a store front in Brooklyn for three months, and I had seen some dance movies including one in which Donald O'Connor tap danced up a wall. I thought that looked like a good thing to do.

The High School of Performing Arts was, if you will, the first "magnet" school for the arts. The interesting thing about it in the 1950s was that the people representing the various dance disciplines on its faculty did not speak to one another. Now they love each other—they not only speak, they even trade repertoire—and I'm not sure how good that is (I 'm becoming a renegade again in my old age). I worked very hard to bring modern dance onto the ballet stage, being the first ballet dancer to dance the works of Jose Limon with American Ballet Theater, my second company. Yet I feel that dance disciplines have a reason for being in and of themselves. When we (ballet dancers) studied modern dance we did so because it was <u>different</u> from what we were accustomed to; it had a different motivation, or way of approaching that which

86

we did. We approached dance in terms of movement originating from the center, in the torso, rather than through a concern for what was happening at the extremities. In fact, we laughed at the French and their overextended, overstretched bodies, those very bodies we have now come to love and admire in world dance.

Why am I telling you this? I will tell you that what you encounter in dance medicine is directly related to what the prevalent technique and style of dance are at any given time. As I see dancers pretzeling themselves out of proportion in very gymnastic ways I wonder what happened to the concept of where movement comes from that was so important to us in the '50s. There is in fact no longer any concern for that kind of thing, so it is time for another revolution. It is time for someone to say "Stop! This is becoming meaningless. More is not necessarily better."

Three weeks ago Sally Wilson arrived in one of these rooms [at the Boston Ballet School] to rehearse Anthony Tudor's "Lilac Garden" with a dancer who shall remain nameless. Every time this great dancer moved around the floor he was showing us his insteps. Sally giggled nervously and said to this dancer, "Dancing Tudor ballets is not about showing us your insteps." In some sense that's where we are now. This is not a tirade against contemporary ballet and modern dance; it is a simple statement of fact that as the technique changes, as our values change, so do the problems.

I think that before this millennium ends another revolution will take place; we will "take our foot off our ear" and start talking again about the importance of the torso. I am trying to do that, to teach dancers where each ballet comes from in movement terms. I am trying to counteract the tendency of ballets to become homogenized with modern dance. It is time to put up some borders and define what dance is again. As a director I take that as one of my missions.

Another of my missions is to create the environment in which this company can work. Balanchine did that in the 1940s and '50s, and it had a widespread effect; his image of the ideal dancer's "look" is still with us. I think worldwide the psyche of the dancer is struggling with the dictum that dancers should not read books; they should not educate themselves; they should work at becoming instruments of the choreographer's vision.

The artistic director also sets the tone of the relationship of the dancer to his/her own body. Traditionally this tone has been, "You must continue at all costs," "You must not pay attention to injury," "The show must go on" even though the dancer need not go on with his/her career. I don't believe that; I have never believed that. There is a temptation to say "Go on anyway. Do it anyway," but I resist that, and I assume other directors do as well.

Last but not least, I believe it is necessary to create a psychological environment wherein it is permissible for a dancer to make a mistake— to have a bad performance. In skiing they say "If you are not falling down you are not learning anything." I think that is true of dancers too. I like to encourage risk-taking in dancers; I like to let them know that one performance isn't all. The important element in the relationship of the artistic director to his dancers is that of encouraging growth.

Role of the Dance Teacher, *Martha Myers, M.S.*

Over the past decade the concept of injury prevention in dance has broadened far beyond knowing where the first aid kit is kept in the studio or what number to call in case of an emergency. The dance teacher has become the first line of defense in an escalating war on injury.

With this expanded role the teacher's responsibilities become far more complex. He/she must understand not only the craft of the art—its technique and artistry—but also (a) how the body works, in terms of anatomy and kinesiology and motor development, and (b) basic concepts of psychological development, especially the psychodynamic issues that pertain to the aspiring professional dancer. Further, (c) the teacher must be able to impart this knowledge to others, and in such a way as to inspire and nurture growth.

Let us briefly consider each of these teaching mandates. As regards mastery of the craft, we are unfortunately still far from realizing the ideal; one can point a finger in any direction and find teachers who are inexperienced and undertrained. Nor can one assume that a great performing artist will be a great teacher; these tasks require equal but different skills.

The teacher must be capable of explaining not only <u>what</u> is to be done, but <u>why</u>. In satisfying this requirement imagery can be very helpful, especially when based in anatomy. This in turn is related to the teacher's need to be able to recognize basic structural patterns in the student, such as hip anteversion, tibial torsion, and scoliosis. With this kind of awareness, students can be guided to the medical advice and possible interventions they may need to continue their dancing fruitfully.

Most dance teachers have developed strong observational skills, often honed on training in body therapies and movement analysis. Their eye immediately records the tightening of neck muscles, unwanted shifts of weight, small and fleeting imperfections of line and quality of motion. These are often not just aesthetic matters; they may point to malalignment or dysfunctional movement patterns, which over time can predispose to injury. A simple example is the practice of holding the arms behind the shoulder girdle in second position, which can be indicative of tight and/or weak rhomboids and of a lordotic lumbar spine. Such a seemingly innocent placement pattern invites problems in both spine and knees.

Highly repetitive motions such as those practiced in dance and sports often lead to overuse injuries. The teacher must recognize patterns of overuse common to the particular form and style of dance he/she teaches, e.g., the emphasis on plantar flexion as opposed to dorsiflexion in ballet or spinal flexion as opposed to hyperextension in much modern dance. Understanding these differences allows the teacher to provide recuperative movement, and address possible muscular imbalances. It acknowledges the validity of a plurality of styles, rather than labeling some "good" and others "bad."

A relatively new factor in overuse syndromes has surfaced with emerging data concerning older athletes and dancers. As careers and life have been extended, so the concept of "overuse" must be re-examined in a framework embracing present practice and long-range survival of body parts. This will have increasing significance for the training of professionals.

Central both to the psychological component of effective teaching and to the question of how information is conveyed in class is the concept of self-care. In *The Science of Dance Training* , Skrinar and Clarkson delineate a variety of "authoritarian behaviors" that, alas, are all too common in dance classes, dictating everything from appropriate wearing apparel to acceptable aesthetic standards. This type of teacher behavior, they say, "is very important when skill acquisition is the primary focus. But when the development of creativity or independent thinking is valued, this form of direct teaching becomes an interference." Such reports should give us pause in considering ways to teach young dancers how to care for themselves, with regard to both their psychological and physical well-being. This has particular implications for developing creative talent.

The teacher must have the eye to tease out <u>what</u> is happening in class and performance, and a storehouse of knowledge from which to do a quick "computer search" for the <u>why</u>— those central components of structure and function that create errors in technique, compromise its aesthetic or expressive values, and predispose to injury. Further, and perhaps most important, the teacher must approach the job of teaching with an awareness that assuming responsibility for another's body/mind is a trust and challenge of the first order.

Life and Training of a Professional Dancer in the United States, *Elaine Bauer*

What characteristics are unique in the dancer who is looking to succeed in a professional career in the United States? First and foremost is the ability to choose; such a career is equally open to everyone. We do not preselect people who wish to study dance on any level here. Second, you must be self-motivated to succeed; I like to think of this in terms of having a survival instinct. And third, you have to be versatile enough to encompass roles in a wide-ranging repertory. This all points to the need for an educational system that takes the whole person into account.

Ballet training in this country tends to begin around age

eight. There is very little guidance available to parents in choosing a school for their children, as we have no form of teacher certification; anyone can open a dance school. The beginning student normally takes two classes per week, each lasting from an hour to an hour and a half. As age increases, so does the number of classes per week. By age 15 the serious student may well be studying six days per week, and the large number of beginning students has been very much reduced. There are educational institutions for children in this age group that have undertaken the merger of general education and preprofessional dance training (such as Walnut Hill School in the Boston area); some professional companies have also done this. The School of American Ballet, for example, sends its students to the High School of Performing Arts. Boston Ballet Company is planning an academy within its soon to be completed Center for Dance Education.

Auditioning is the process by which people get jobs with professional companies in this country, and it normally coincides with graduation from high school. This can continue for several years and is often very difficult for young people who are also faced with other life choices, such as going to college. For a ballet dancer, the first few years in a company usually constitute his/her "higher education."

Most ballet dancers enter the company at the level of *corps de ballet;* very few get soloist or principal contracts right away, but there is usually every opportunity to work one's way up.

The aspects of life in a ballet company that most directly impact upon the possibility of dance injury are layoffs, tours, and diversity of repertory. Although companies try to have a consistent contract period, layoffs are inevitable. The number depends on the budget and the availability of work. Dancers do not take vacations. They must have the initiative to sustain themselves through this time.

Tours take dancers out of their usual environment, into rehearsal and performance spaces that are often inadequate. The chance for injury increases with the length of the tour, the amount of time spent in each city, and the difficulty of the repertory. Diversity of repertory and its effect on dance injuries is unique to ballet companies, especially those in the United States. The repertory of these companies spans literally every period and idiom, from the romantic ballets of the nineteenth century to the most *avant garde* of today. The classically trained body is not always prepared to make switches from the classical to the modern idiom and back within the short amount of rehearsal time allowed.

The length of a typical ballet career varies widely depending on many factors, most importantly, how the body holds up. There are no retirement plans in ballet; when you choose no longer to do this thing, you are on your own. I have just taken the step into retirement myself within this last year. Some of the things I have noticed are that I can wear my glasses in public, that I have purchased a business suit, and that I give many lectures.

Dance Training in the Soviet Union: Experiences of an American Student and Performer, *Anna-Marie Holmes*

I actually began my training in the Soviet system in Vancouver, Canada, and went from there to the Soviet Union where I trained and danced with the Kirov Ballet. The first thing that the Russian teachers did when I arrived in Leningrad was to make me very aware of my stomach. They said that was the center of my body, the source of my strength, and that was what I needed to focus on. They would literally come up and punch me in the stomach, which wasn't great fun, especially when I didn't understand the language or much of what was happening.

After about six months there I took a teaching course, which greatly increased my understanding of why the Russian teachers did things. I would like to say something in this context about Vagonova (to whom I had a direct connection through the fact that my principal teacher in the Soviet Union was the person who succeeded her). Vagonova training made me very aware of being square; everything in the body was placed squarely on the legs; everything in alignment was straight. I think this was responsible for the fact that I had an injury-free career; learning to make the leg muscles pull up into the body and have a strong stomach center point saved me. I also found later in my career that I could go into jazz and modern work because I had this strong focal point. The teachers I studied with in Russia felt that you need not only the strong center in the stomach but also great plasticity in the arms. Expressiveness should come through the upper body. They thought the Cecchetti legs were good, but the arms were too rigid. They liked the softness of the Fokine arms. So basically they combined the Cecchetti leg with the Fokine arm.

The Soviet training system is now eight years in length, and students normally start with it at age ten. They tried a six-year system, but decided ultimately that as they have the time there (with state support) they might as well stick with the safer eight years.

The children take an hour and a half of ballet every day in the first three years, plus 45 minutes of historical dancing. In the fourth year they add character dancing, which is harder on the legs. They tend to develop quite a bit of flexibility in the legs; if there happens to be some pronation they try to correct it, but they allow a flexibility with the ankle and the knee to the extent that some people really argue with it. The supporters of this practice argue that allowing some rolling over strengthens the muscles around the joints. The last four years they introduce easy stretching on the floor for the children before the class begins. After the fifth year the men begin to have different training; they work with different tempos, lighter jumps, etc.

Questions and Answers: *Panel Members*

Question: What kind of art-related experience should be offered to young dancers in order to round out their development?

Martha Myers: At least Eurythmics, and folk dance, and both structured and free play.

Anna-Marie Holmes: Yes, play is certainly important. The very young Russian students take two months off in the summer, and they are encouraged to use that as play time— with some emphasis on swimming for the muscles.

Elaine Bauer: I agree with the need for children in the eight to twelve year old group to have time away from dance, though in this country the summer tends to be a time for intensified training because, as we have said, throughout the school year you are having to balance dance training with regular school activities. The Boston Ballet School has a summer program, which we use to really focus our students in on dance, but we do introduce types of work there—in modern, jazz, and character—that vary the tempo and keep it light. We also expose the summer students to a good deal of dance on video, to broaden their perspective. We give them classes in music, stage design, costume, etc., so they begin to understand that there is more to theater than just being in class and doing *pliés.* We also bring in members of the physical therapy staff from Children's Hospital to begin teaching them care of their bodies.

Anna-Marie Holmes: I think music education is very important for young dancers.

Question: What about sports?

Anna-Marie Holmes: Swimming is awfully good, and of course team sports. There are two theories about sports: Some feel they are good for developing the leg muscles; others worry about the injury potential.

Question: I wonder about the teaching of composition and the mind-broadening of young students that goes along with it. Are you addressing this issue?

Bruce Marks: We will be addressing it soon. We at the Boston Ballet are in the process of building a new 60,000 square foot facility in the South End of Boston. It will be a Center for Dance Education, which is essentially a new concept. We are very cognizant that in the United States less and less money is going into the arts; it is increasingly the responsibility of each art form, therefore, to look out for itself. So our energies are turning to becoming an educational organization for our region. We will begin to educate not only <u>in</u> dance, but <u>about</u>

dance. One of the exciting things about the new service program is that it will provide ballet students what modern dance students have traditionally enjoyed—the opportunity to create. We know we must encourage those working in the balletic idiom to create dance. Once we begin to do that I assure you we will again have many choreographers working in ballet in America.

Martha Myers: That raises a point I wasn't able to develop earlier, which has to do with "authoritarian teaching." A lot is being written about this subject now, and there are about ten points that define it: telling the student what to wear, where to stand, when to start dancing and when to stop, what is aesthetically pleasing and what is not, etc. This approach to teaching obviously does not promote individual thinking and creativity. That is why I mentioned the need for free play in the training of dancers. There is also something called "body therapies," which is the study of movement, repatterning, and creativity all put together; it complements the composition, which has its origins in improvisation.

Question: Do you see any injury patterns, such as arthritis, that are especially prevalent in older or ex-dancers?

William Hamilton: There simply isn't enough research to prove anything one way or another on that. We need to see whether it isn't faults in early training that produce injuries 20 or 30 years later.

Lyle Micheli: The research in sports medicine is similarly inconclusive.

Question *(Iris Fanger):* I direct the summer dance program based at Harvard each year, and because we are in one of the major medical centers of the world we are able to provide our students with excellent medical assistance and advice. I get the sense, though, that this is not the case in many other parts of the country.

Martha Myers: Because our summer program (American

Dance Festival) is based in Durham, North Carolina, we work very closely with Duke University Medical Center, especially with their physical therapists. They provide not only care for our students, but also an excellent screening program to help foresee problems and thereby assist students in coping with the rigors of an intensive summer of dance. I know that experimental work is being done with screening at the University of California, Irvine, and I think this kind of thing is badly needed.

Lyle Micheli: We will be starting a five-year prospective program next fall to screen and follow students at the Boston Ballet School. Yes, this kind of thing is a big problem nationwide. The American College of Sports Medicine will have Dr. Bill Hamilton at its convention in Salt Lake City next week to talk to those doctors and basically bring them up to speed on special problems in dancers.

Question/Statement: I notice a lack of discussion here, and I suspect in the field generally, of how dance companies can incorporate work in such therapies as acupuncture and massage. I think, for example, it could be very beneficial for a ballet company to have a massage therapist available at all times.

Bruce Marks: I thoroughly agree with you. The only problem is money: Money tends to dictate the reality of what a company can do. I am happy to report that the new Boston Ballet facility will have both physical therapy and physical training rooms. We have budgeted funds so that a year from now our dancers will have a full range of preventive and rehabilitative care available to them. I think we will be in the forefront of the field in that respect.

Anna-Marie Holmes: The Russians are very good about providing the care you suggest. If a student so much as flinches in class they are immediately sent to the therapy room.

Lyle Micheli: The usefulness of massage in dealing with

dance injuries really has not been studied. We all know it makes you feel good, but we aren't sure exactly how useful it is. In particular it has not been scientifically demonstrated that massage is helpful in the prevention of dance injuries, yet many practitioners state this, as if it were a proven fact. I would be fascinated to see a study of that.

4

QUESTIONS AND ANSWERS

Questions and Answers

Following the Presentations of William Hamilton, M.D., Linda Hamilton, Ph.D., and Elly Trepman, M.D.

Question (to Trepman): In the study of stress fractures in the military, where were the fractures located?

Trepman: The study was of the Israeli army, which had about a 30% stress fracture rate. The fractures were mainly in the tibia. The foot fractures were inevitably in the metatarsals.

William Hamilton: There may be at least a distant connection between that problem and stress fractures in dancers. As Linda [Hamilton] mentioned, when dancers are having weight problems we think to give them some exercise to do, like running (otherwise they are likely to get caught up in eating disorders). But dancers make terrible runners; they are so turned out, so duck footed, they run in external tibial torsion, which may be conducive to the same kind of injuries encountered by the Israeli soldiers. So it is better to give dancers other kinds of supplemental exercises for weight control, like swimming.

Question: Couldn't schools and companies have programs for the vocational guidance of dancers and ex-dancers?

Linda Hamilton: Yes they could, and they are starting. The dancers at the New York City Ballet, for example, are organizing and have seminars yearly to discuss this kind of thing.

What we are finding, though, is an inherent passivity in dancers, a lack of initiative, an unwillingness to take control of their lives.

William Hamilton: But that is changing too. People are paying attention to this problem now. It isn't right to say it is totally neglected any more.

Question: How do dancers, especially modern dancers, get appropriate information about and care for their injuries? Are there monetary resources they can draw on?

William Hamilton: If you go to the sports medicine conferences now you will find that, unlike ten years ago, there are papers being given on dance injuries. So the word is getting out that way. In the smaller cities there usually aren't enough dancers to justify having a dance specialist around, but there are enough athletes to have a sports medicine clinic, and the people there are increasingly prepared to deal with dancers. As to monetary resources, that is tied in with workers' compensation, which is different in every state.

Question: What do you recommend for educating dancers nutritionally?

Linda Hamilton: Many dance companies are sponsoring seminars in this area.

Question: What modalities do you recommend for preventing injuries, especially in male dancers?

William Hamilton: The young dancer with the right body probably doesn't need to do anything. As they get older, though, they may need some extra conditioning to stay in shape, and the dancer returning from injury definitely needs that. I think the Pilates equipment is excellent for use in these cases. We found out some time ago that male dancers are generally weak in the upper body, so they should be put routinely on weight training, even before they start partnering.

Lyle Micheli: Yes, but the problem we find with strength training, whether with Pilates, or weights, or whatever, is compliance. It is not hard to provide the means for developing strength, but it is very difficult to get dancers to stick to a strength training program.

Elly Trepman: As regards getting back into dance after an injury: For every day you are inactive you have to rehab for at least two days, so if you are in a cast for three or four weeks we are talking about three months to get back to full form. Anything you can do during that interval to maintain aerobic fitness and strength elsewhere in your body is highly worthwhile.

William Hamilton: We do that routinely; whenever a dancer is put in a cast they are immediately sent to the Pilates room.

Question: Do you find any correlation between "burn-out" and retirement?

Linda Hamilton: No, in the dancers we have studied the only factor that causes a dancer to consider retirement is age.

William Hamilton: That tends to be different in Europe, where state subsidies allow companies to keep dancers on well beyond their active performing age. At the Paris Ballet, for example, only a small percentage of the company actually performs.

Question: Can you give the criteria on which the EAT-26 test for evaluating anorexia is based?

Linda Hamilton: They have identified three subscales: oral control, bulimia, and purging. Those are characteristics of deviant eating disorders, but you couldn't use those scales in diagnosis. In addition to the deviant behavior, you need weight loss and amenorrhea to confirm a diagnosis of anorexia.

Question: In our discussions here we have been focusing on large, urban-based dance schools and companies, but how do you get the kind of information they need to teachers throughout the country?

Lyle Micheli: The answer is certification. There are now three national organizations for educating and certifying sports coaches. The same must be done in dance—but who will do it?

Martha Myers: The National Dance Association and the American Dance Guild are working on this. It is interesting that the newest form of dance, aerobics, has done the most with certification—and education.

William Hamilton: In all fairness, the picture with regard to injuries may not be as bleak as we make it out to be at conferences like this. Serious injuries are really quite rare; dance is one of the safest sports.

Question: Do you see different health patterns in dancers who have come up through college programs than in the subculture of professional dancers you have studied?

Linda Hamilton: I have only focused on the isolated subculture, but having met many modern dancers who went to college and started dancing at a later age, I certainly think I see many differences. They seem much more rounded, better educated, many of them are married, and they do better when they leave the profession than ballet dancers do.

Question: Does coming out of college preclude a professional career?

Linda Hamilton: Yes. If you haven't gotten into a large national company by the age of 20 no one is going to take you. But I will say it is possible for ballet dancers, especially near the end of their career, to take college courses, and even work toward degrees.

5

PRESENTERS

PRESENTERS

Elaine Bauer was a principal dancer with the Boston Ballet from 1971 to 1989, during which time she danced most of the major roles in the ballet repertory (including several opposite Rudolph Nureyev). In addition to her performing career, Ms. Bauer has taught at the University of Louisville, Boston Conservatory, Butler University, Jordan College of Music, and the Boston Ballet School. She recently received an Honorary Doctor of Fine Arts Degree from her alma mater, Butler University, "in recognition of her contribution to the art form."

Priscilla M. Clarkson, Ph.D., is associate professor in the Department of Exercise Science at the University of Massachusetts. Her wide-ranging service to the field includes chairing committees for such organizations as the American Alliance for Health, Physical Education, Recreation and Dance and the American College of Sports Medicine; she is also a reviewer for *The Physician and Sportsmedicine, JAMA,* and various other periodicals. Prof. Clarkson is co-editor (with Margaret Skrinar) of *The Science of Dance Training* (1988) and co-author (with Andrea Watkins) of *Strength Conditioning for Dancers* (1990).

Linda Hamilton, Ph.D., a former dancer with the New York City Ballet, is now a clinical psychologist (and teacher of undergraduate psychology at Fordham University) with specialties in eating disorders and performing arts psychology. Her most recent publication (*American Journal of Sports Medicine,* Spring, 1989) deals with "Personality, Stress, and Injuries in Professional Ballet Dancers." She has recently returned from the USSR, where she studied eating disorders of the Kirov dancers.

William G. Hamilton, M.D., is assistant clinical professor of orthopaedic surgery at Columbia University College of Physicians and Surgeons in New York City. He serves as orthopaedic surgeon to the New York City Ballet, the School of American Ballet, and American Ballet Theater, and as orthopaedic consultant to numerous other ballet and modern companies, including the Alvin Ailey American Dance Theater. Dr. Hamilton is very widely published and a frequent presenter, in the field of dance medicine. He also sits on various administrative and editorial boards.

Anna-Marie Holmes is assistant to the director and, since 1985, ballet mistress of the Boston Ballet. As a ballerina she appeared in more than 30 countries on five continents, and she was the first North American to be invited to perform with the Kirov Ballet in Russia. She is recognized worldwide for her interpretations of the great Russian classics, which she has produced or set on companies in London, Lisbon, Rome, Montreal, and New York. Ms. Holmes has appeared frequently on television and in dance films, for which she has won such awards as First Prize American Film Festival, Grand Prix Cannes Festival, and Premier Prix Prague Film Festival.

Bruce Marks has had a distinguished career as dancer, director, and choreographer with the Metropolitan Opera Ballet, American Ballet Theater, and Ballet West. In 1985 he assumed his current role as artistic director of the Boston Ballet. Mr. Marks has been very active in behalf of the National Endowment for the Arts, helping, for example, to establish its National Choreography Program. He is chairman of the 1990 USA Jackson International Ballet Competition and was a judge at the Moscow International Ballet Competition in 1989.

Lyle J. Micheli, M.D., is director of sports medicine at Children's Hospital and associate clinical professor of orthopaedic surgery with Harvard Medical School, both located in Boston. He is president of the American College of Sports Medicine and has been attending physician for the Boston Ballet Company and medical consultant to the Boston Ballet School for the past 13 years. Dr. Micheli is the author of over 100 scientific articles related to sports injuries and the medical problems of dancers, and serves on the advisory and editorial boards of numerous publications.

Sergei Mironov, M.D., is head, section of Sports, Dance, Circus, Performance Medicine, Central Institute of Orthopaedics and Traumatology, Moscow, USSR. He is also head physician to the Soviet Union Olympic Team, and Soviet delegate to the Federation Internationale de Medicine Sportive (FIMS). Dr. Mironov came to the United States as head of the six-person Soviet delegation (sponsored by the National Institutes of Health) to a bi-national conference on dance injuries held May 1990 in Bethesda, Maryland.

Martha Myers, M.S., is dean of the American Dance Festival and professor of dance at Connecticut College. She has a wide range of credits as teacher, dancer, choreographer, television performer, writer, and dance/ movement consultant. At ADF she directs and teaches in the Center for Professional Dance Training and Education, which presents workshops on the body therapies, dance medicine, and choreography. She has taught and lectured across this country and in Europe, Japan, South America, and Australia. Ms. Myers' articles on the body therapies and dance injury prevention have appeared in numerous dance publications.

Christine Ploski, P.T., M.S., has been in practice as a physical therapist for 14 years. She currently is an assistant supervisor in the Department of Physical Therapy at Children's Hospital in Boston. She has a wide range of experience with both the pediatric and adult populations and has been concerned with dance medicine for ten years. She is actively involved in rehabilitation of dance injuries and has a special interest in the education of young dancers in the areas of anatomy and injury prevention.

Daniel S. Rooks, Sc.D., is clinical exercise physiologist in the Division of Sports Medicine and research scientist in the Department of Orthopaedic Surgery at Children's Hospital, Boston. He is also a lecturer at Boston University.

Ruth Solomon has been a distinguished performer and choreographer in the modern dance idiom for many years. She is also a dance educator of note, having directed the dance program at the University of California, Santa Cruz since 1970. Her teaching technique is documented in the award-winning video, "Anatomy as a Master Image in Training Dancers" (1988). She is widely published in the literature of both dance and medicine, including her recent book, *Preventing Dance Injuries: An Interdisciplinary Perspective* (AAHPERD Publications, 1990).

Elly Trepman, M.D., was a clinical fellow in orthopaedic surgery, Harvard Medical School (1984-88), resident in orthopaedic surgery, Harvard Combined Orthopaedic Program (1984-87), chief resident, Orthopaedic Surgery, Brigham and Women's Hospital (Boston, 1987), and fellow in sports medicine at Children's Hospital in Boston (1988). He is currently assistant professor of orthopaedics and rehabilitation at the Yale University School of Medicine in New Haven. His dance-related publications have appeared in *Kinesiology and Medicine for Dance* and *Preventing Dance Injuries: An Interdisciplinary Perspective.*

Chris Troyanos, A.C.T., is head athletic trainer for the Babson College athletic teams and sports medicine consultant to the Boston Bolts Soccer Club. He is also owner/director of Charles River Sports Therapy West in Wellesley, Mass., and Sports Medicine Consultant, Inc. For 12 years he served as medical coordinator of the Boston Marathon Finish Line Medical Team, supervising the efforts of 350 doctors, nurses, athletic trainers and physical therapists.

Arleen Walaszek is a physical therapist with clinical expertise in pediatric and adult orthopaedics. She has been in practice for 16 years, serving as the physical therapy consultant to the Boston Ballet since 1978 and on the staff of Children's Hospital, Boston, since 1986. She has lectured widely on the prevention and rehabilitation of dance injuries. Her training in this field includes work with Ruth Solomon's anatomical approach to training dancers, and the Alexander Technique.

Ellen Wallach is a career development consultant, professional speaker, author, and film maker. For the past 16 years she has designed career management programs and human resource systems for business, industrial, educational, and governmental clients, including the Pacific Northwest Ballet. In 1988 she completed a three-year research study of former professional dancers: "Life After Performing: Career Transitions for Dancers." This project was undertaken in response to a request from the National Endowment for the Arts, which funded the effort.

PHOTO CREDITS